THE FOUNDER'S FORMULA

—·—

AI, ENTREPRENEURSHIP AND GROWTH FROM START TO EXIT

MARK LOUDERMILK

PHOENIX & SAGE
PUBLISHING

PHOENIX & SAGE

First Edition

ISBN: 979-8-9987658-0-3

Self-published by Mark Loudermilk

Cover design by Phoenix & Sage Publishing

This book is designed to provide accurate and authoritative information on the topics covered. It is sold with the understanding that neither the author nor the publisher is engaged in rendering legal, accounting, or other professional services. If expert assistance is required, the services of a competent professional should be sought.

The stories, experiences, and examples shared in this book are based on the author's real-life experiences and observations. Some names and identifying details have been changed to protect the privacy of individuals.

Success in business, as in life, is the result of preparation, hard work,learning from failure, loyalty, and persistence. This book provides guidance,but results will vary based on numerous factors specific to your situation.

To those who believe in second chances—especially when those chances must be given to ourselves.
And to every entrepreneur with the courage to build something from nothing, even when the path seems impossible.

PREFACE

In the fall of 2017, I found myself standing in an empty warehouse in Brooklyn, staring at my phone as the first transaction of my third startup pinged through. It wasn't the largest sum of money—just $497 for a software license—but the sound of that notification represented something profound: the moment when an idea transforms into reality.

That transformation—from concept to company, from vision to execution—is what this book is about.

Entrepreneurship has changed dramatically in the last few years. The rise of artificial intelligence, the democratization of powerful tools, and the evolution of funding models have created an entirely new landscape for founders. Today, a single person with the right mindset can accomplish what once required entire teams. A startup can scale globally from day one. Market insights that once took months to gather can now be assembled in hours.

But one thing hasn't changed: **building something meaningful is still incredibly hard**.

Despite all our technological advantages, most new ventures still fail. Founders still face dark nights of the soul, questioning everything. Teams still fracture under pressure. The fundamentals of value creation, problem-solving, and human connection remain as critical as ever.

I wrote *The Founder's Formula* because I believe that success in this new era requires both timeless wisdom and cutting-edge tools. My own journey—from a troubled youth to building and selling multiple companies across healthcare and technology—has taught me that entrepreneurship is as much about who you become as what you build.

This isn't just another business book filled with platitudes. It's a comprehensive blueprint built from hard-won lessons—some learned through triumph, others through painful failure. Within these pages, you'll find practical frameworks, tactical advice, and strategic insights that span the entire entrepreneurial journey:

- How to break free from limiting beliefs and develop the mindset of a successful founder

- Practical techniques for generating and validating business ideas

- Step-by-step guidance on legal structures and incorporation decisions

- Advanced strategies for leveraging AI throughout your business

- Frameworks for raising capital and planning potential exits

But more than tactics, this book is about transformation. It's about how the entrepreneurial path—with all its challenges and victories—shapes not just your business but your character. It's about building something that matters while becoming someone who makes a difference.

Whether you're contemplating your first startup or scaling your fifth, my hope is that this book serves as both compass and companion on your journey. The world needs builders who combine ambition with integrity, innovation with purpose. The world needs you and your ideas.

The path ahead won't be easy. But as I've discovered through my own ventures, the most valuable things rarely are.

It's time to begin.

Mark Loudermilk – Spring 2025

INTRODUCTION

The Blueprint for Transformation

"The true measure of success is not how much you get, but how much you give back."

This simple truth has guided my entrepreneurial journey from the beginning—a journey that started in the most unexpected of places and led to building multiple successful businesses across healthcare, technology, and beyond. What I've learned along the way is that entrepreneurship, at its core, isn't about chasing wealth. It's about solving problems that matter and creating value for others.

Think about this: If your first question when starting a business is "How can I get rich?", you're already on the wrong path. But if you begin by asking, "How can I genuinely help others?", you've discovered the true foundation of sustainable success. Fortune follows service—not the other way around.

In this book, we'll explore the complete arc of building a meaningful business, from personal transformation to practical execution to potential exit. I call this "The Founder's Formula"—a blend of philosophical wisdom and cutting-edge strategies that can guide you through every stage of the entrepreneurial journey.

My own path wasn't conventional. As you'll discover in the first chapters, my journey began in confinement—both physical and mental—where I was forced to confront my limitations and re-imagine what was possible. Those hard-won lessons became the foundation for everything that followed: multiple businesses, successful exits, and the opportunity to mentor others along the way.

"Your history is not your destiny. Your choices today create your reality tomorrow."

This philosophy transformed my life and my approach to business. Working for decades in emergency rooms and ICUs as a nurse and respiratory therapist, I witnessed daily how fragile life can be—and how resilient the human spirit is.Those lessons in the hospital transferred seamlessly to entrepreneurship: stay calm under pressure, make decisions with limited information, and always prioritize the needs of those you serve.

Later, when building Treydora as a AAA game and educational platform, I applied another principle: "Technology without purpose is just distraction; technology with purpose is transformation." Every venture I've undertaken has been guided by asking not "What can I build?" but rather "What should I build that makes lives better?"

Throughout these pages, you'll find both inspiration and practical instruction. Whether you're starting with nothing but a dream, figuring out your company's legal structure, seeking funding, implementing AI tools to accelerate growth, or considering taking your company public, you'll discover actionable insights informed by real experience.

"The entrepreneurial path isn't about avoiding failures—it's about failing forward, learning quickly, and persisting despite setbacks."

This journey is neither straight nor easy. There will be days when you question everything, when obstacles seem insurmountable. I've been there. But with the right mindset, the right knowledge, and the right tools,entrepreneurship can be one of the most rewarding journeys you'll ever undertake. This book aims to be your companion along the way—offering both the philosophical perspective to weather the storms and the tactical know-how to navigate the waters.

Founder's Insight: "Great businesses aren't built by accident—they're built through intention. Every day, choose to be deliberate about the company you're creating, the people you're serving, and the leader you're becoming."

Let's begin building something that matters—not just for ourselves, but for those we have the privilege to serve.

"The businesses that last aren't built on trends or tricks—they're built on truth, trust, and genuine value."

In the chapters ahead, we'll walk through every stage of the entrepreneurial journey. We'll start where all true success begins—with personal transformation—and then build outward to the practical tools and strategies that will help you translate your vision into reality. The path won't always be easy, but as you'll soon discover, the most worthwhile journeys rarely are.

CONTENTS

1

BREAKING THE CHAINS WITHIN

The heavy **clang** of the steel door echoed as it shut behind me. In that moment, the world I knew fell away—replaced by a six-by-eight-foot prison cell that felt colder than ice. I sank onto the hard cot, head in my hands, wondering how my life had come to this point. I was nineteen years old and *this* was rock bottom. Shame and regret settled on my shoulders like a yoke. Yet amid the despair, a stubborn spark refused to die out inside me.

I realized I had a choice: I could let this prison sentence break me, or I could use it to remake myself. As Friedrich Nietzsche once observed, *"To live is to suffer, to survive is to find some meaning in the suffering."* His words rang in my mind on those darkest nights. If I was going to survive here—truly *survive* in spirit, not just in body—I had to find meaning in this misery. I had to turn this rock bottom into the solid foundation for a new life.

Founder's Truth: "Your lowest point can become your strongest foundation. It's not what happens to you, but how you transform what happens that determines your destiny."

Gray dawn light crept through the barred window each morning as I resolved to transform my routine. Instead of staring at the ceiling and cursing my fate, I started **owning my days** in whatever way I could. I began to wake up before dawn for quiet meditation and push-ups on the concrete floor. I volunteered for the prison library job, carting books to other inmates—anything to keep my mind engaged.

One sweltering afternoon organizing dusty bookshelves, I stumbled on a tattered copy of Marcus Aurelius's *Meditations*. I'd never heard of this Roman emperor-philosopher, but as I flipped through the brittle pages, one passage stopped me cold: *"You have power over your mind—not outside events. Realize this, and you will find strength."* I read those words over and over. Aurelius was telling me that while I couldn't control **being** in prison, I could control **how** I responded to it. My situation didn't have to define me—*my mindset could.*

That idea hit me like a lightning bolt in the darkness. I decided then and there to take ownership of my future, even behind bars.

That night, in the dim light of my cell, I made myself a promise. I looked into the scratched metal mirror above the tiny sink, met my own hardened gaze, and whispered: *"My past may have led me here, but it will not dictate where I go from here. I own my mistakes, and I will own my future."* In that moment I felt a strange surge of freedom—**inside** a prison of all places. I had stumbled upon a powerful truth: the greatest prison is not made of concrete and steel, but of a limited mind. And I now held the key to my own mental cell.

Transformation Truth: "When you're unable to change your environment, focus on changing yourself. The knowledge you gain, the skills you build, and the discipline you develop become portable assets no one can take from you."

With this new mindset, I attacked each day with purpose. I enrolled in every educational program available. First was earning my GED—the high school diploma I'd neglected to get on the outside. I spent late nights hunched over textbooks, turning a cramped cell into a classroom. When I passed the exam and held that certificate in my hand, I felt *pride* for the first time in ages. It was a small step, but a crucial one.

Next, I signed up for a distance-learning college course in psychology, borrowing every textbook I could find. I became **obsessed with learning**, as if knowledge were my lifeline pulling me out of a swift undertow. I devoured books on history, business, philosophy—anything I could get. Between shifts mopping floors or working in the kitchen, I'd be scribbling notes on vocabulary or math formulas. Other inmates would see my nose buried in a book and joke, "What, you studying to be a lawyer or something?" I'd just smile and keep reading. In truth, I *was* studying to be something—I was studying to be **better** than the man who walked into this place.

Of course, there were setbacks. Some days, the weight of where I was—and how far I had to go—felt crushing. I remember prison riots kicking off and that old frustration flare up. For a moment, I heard a nagging voice: *"Who are you kidding? You're a criminal, not a college kid."* During lockdowns I paced my cell, wrestling with doubt. But instead of giving up, I recalled why I started. I thought of the day I was arrested, the disappointment in my mother's eyes when she saw me in an orange jumpsuit. I let that memory fuel me rather than shame me.

Failure, I decided, was not going to be the end of my story—it would be *the plot twist* that made my comeback possible. I was learning one of life's great truths: a failure is only final if you stop trying. So I continued my pathway one step at a time. Each small victory—each passed exam, each completed book—was proof that I was more than my inmate number.

Resilience Revelation: "Every challenge presents two paths—surrender or growth. Choose growth consistently, and eventually, your challenges become your champions."

Over the next three years, I transformed within those prison walls. I became a mentor to younger inmates, encouraging them to join me in the library or to write down goals for life after release. I kept a journal where I mapped out the person I wanted to become: educated, resilient, compassionate, and entrepreneurial. Yes, entrepreneurial—even in prison, I dreamed of starting a business one day, of building something positive and **proving that my past could fuel a brighter future**.

Every time negativity or bitterness crept in, I returned to the insight I'd gained: *focus on what you can control and let go of what you can't.* I couldn't control the length of my sentence or the noise of my cell block at night. But I *could* control whether I studied an extra hour, whether I treated others with respect, whether I kept my hope alive. That mindset became my armor.

The morning I finally walked out of those gates, I clutched a small duffel bag filled with letters, books, and the certificates I earned. The sun on my face felt like a warm welcome to a new world. Three years earlier I had arrived in shackles, hopeless. Now I stepped out a different man: educated, determined, and **hungry for a second chance**. I had entered prison a prisoner, but I was leaving it a free man in every sense.

Before me lay an open road—and I vowed to myself I would never waste this freedom I fought so hard for internally. My journey of personal transformation had begun behind bars, but it would continue for a lifetime. As I took my first steps outside, I whispered one more personal mantra under my breath: *"Your history is not your destiny. From today on, I'm the author of my life."* The past was a lesson, not a life sentence. I was ready to write the next chapters with purpose and pride.

The Entrepreneur's First Crucible

Looking back now from the vantage point of success, I can see clearly what I couldn't then: that prison was my first entrepreneurial training ground. The skills that would later build businesses—discipline, strategic thinking, resource optimization, and unwavering focus—were forged in that unlikely crucible. While I would never wish that experience on anyone, I recognize now that transformation rarely happens in comfortable circumstances. It emerges from challenge, from having no choice but to reinvent yourself when old paths are closed to you.

I remember a particular moment during my second year inside. The prison experienced a week-long lockdown after a fight in another block. Confined to our cells 24/7, most inmates grew restless and angry. I decided to use the time differently. With nothing but a pencil stub and the margins of an old newspaper, I sketched out my first crude business plan—a healthcare staffing service that would address the scheduling problems I'd noticed during a previous hospital job. The idea wasn't revolutionary, but the act of creation amid such constraint was powerful. I realized that entrepreneurs don't wait for perfect conditions—they create value regardless of circumstances.

That business plan would eventually become my first successful venture after release. But more importantly, that week taught me that entrepreneurship is fundamentally about resourcefulness—using whatever you have at hand to build something valuable. Whether you're in a prison cell with nothing but a pencil or in a garage with nothing but a computer, the entrepreneurial mindset finds a way forward.

Mindset Maxim: "Every limitation is simply an invitation to innovate. The constraints that feel like barriers today may become the boundaries that focus your greatest strengths tomorrow."

The year after my release, I found myself facing a different kind of confinement—financial constraints while trying to launch my staffing business. With barely enough money for rent, I couldn't afford office space or fancy software. But my prison experience had taught me to work with what I had. I converted a corner of my studio apartment into an office. I used free scheduling software and made up for its limitations with meticulous manual tracking. When I couldn't afford advertising, I walked into hospitals with homemade brochures and spoke directly to nursing directors about their staffing pain points.

My first client—a small rehabilitation center struggling with weekend staffing—signed on not because I had impressive credentials or slick marketing, but because I genuinely understood their problem and offered a solution tailored to their needs. I had lived the constraint of limited resources for so long that finding creative workarounds had become second nature. What others might have seen as disadvantages—my background, limited capital, no business network—I transformed into a different kind of approach that stood out precisely because it wasn't conventional.

When I meet aspiring entrepreneurs who believe they need perfect conditions to start—ideal funding, complete knowledge, or flawless timing—I tell them about those early days. The truth is that building something from nothing is never about having everything you need; it's about making the most of what you have while systematically acquiring what you don't.

Every successful entrepreneur I've met shares this quality—they didn't wait for ideal circumstances; they made progress with the tools at hand while working toward something better. The most valuable asset isn't funding or connections or even experience—it's the ability to start where you are, with what you have, and build something meaningful despite the constraints.

Key Takeaways (Chapter 1)

- **Find Meaning in Adversity:** No matter how painful your situation, look for a purpose within it. As Nietzsche said, finding meaning in your suffering is the key to surviving and growing stronger.

- **Own Your Response:** You can't always control what happens to you, but you *can* control how you respond. Focus on your mindset and actions—that's where your strength lies (a lesson from Stoic philosophy).

- **Start Where You Are:** Don't wait for perfect conditions to begin your transformation. Use whatever resources and time you have right now—even if you're at "rock bottom," you can start building a foundation for change today.

- **Rewrite Your Story: Take ownership** of your life story. Let go of excuses and blaming circumstances. The moment you decide to accept full responsibility for your future, you reclaim the power to change it.

- **Let Failure Fuel You:** Treat setbacks as feedback, not the end. Every failure can teach you something and prime you for a stronger comeback. When you refuse to let setbacks define you, they **refine** you into a more resilient person.

- **Turn Constraints Into Catalysts:** Your limitations are not obstacles to success but catalysts for creativity. The entrepreneur who thrives isn't the one with unlimited resources, but the one who sees opportunity in constraint.

The journey of breaking free from my mental prison was just the first step. Next came the equally challenging process of building a new life and identity. As we move into Chapter 2, you'll see how the foundation of self-transformation became the launchpad for education, skill-building, and eventually, business creation—proving that with enough determination, you can completely reinvent not just who you are, but what you're capable of creating in the world.

2

— . —

DEGREES OF FREEDOM

Stepping back into the free world was both exhilarating and terrifying. I had a second chance—a chance many never get—and I was determined not to squander it. On my first night out, I sat at my small kitchen table (in a cramped apartment generously offered by a cousin) and sketched out a plan for my life on a scrap of paper.

I remembered a powerful piece of advice from motivational speaker Jim Rohn: *"If you don't design your own life plan, chances are you'll fall into someone else's plan. And guess what they have planned for you? Not much."* I took those words to heart. I knew that if I didn't take control of my direction now, old habits or random circumstances would pull me off course. So I became the **architect of my own destiny**, mapping out goals for the next five years: finish a college degree, start a meaningful career, and ultimately build my own business. The page in front of me fluttered in the breeze from the open window, as if urging me forward. I clenched it in my hand with resolve. This was *my* life plan, and I was going to make it real.

Freedom Philosophy: "True freedom isn't about doing whatever you want—it's about disciplining yourself to do what matters most. The paradox of freedom is that it flourishes within deliberate boundaries."

One of my first goals was to pursue an education in healthcare. During my time inside, I had discovered a fascination with health and healing—partly from devouring biology textbooks, and partly from helping the prison nurse on first-aid duty. I chose **Respiratory Therapy** as my path forward. Respiratory appealed to me because it was a chance to help others heal and to prove to myself that I could be a caregiver, a positive force.

But going from ex-inmate to registered respiratory therapist was no simple leap. I enrolled in a community college for prerequisite courses, and on day one, at age 20, I walked into a classroom for the first time as a free man. I felt out of place. My background was different than most students and certainly more rough around the edges. In the back of my mind lurked the fear that my criminal record would define me in everyone's eyes. But if I had learned anything, it was that the only way to change people's perceptions was through my actions and excellence. **I hit the ground running.**

The Freedom of Discipline

Balancing work, study, and personal responsibilities was my next big challenge. To support myself through school, I took a job as a dishwasher at a local restaurant in the evenings. I'd finish class in the afternoon, head straight to work scrubbing pots and pans until late night, then come home and crack open the books to study. It was exhausting, but I had a mission driving me forward.

Time was no longer something I had in excess (like in prison); it was a precious resource I had to manage relentlessly. I remembered another piece of Jim Rohn's wisdom: *"Either you run the day, or the day runs you."* So I learned to **run my days** with almost military discipline. I woke up at 5:00 AM to review notes or get a quick workout in, knowing that physical health kept my mind sharp. I carried flashcards to quiz myself during my lunch break. I even recorded lectures on my phone to play back during my commute. Every hour was accounted for.

This rigorous time management wasn't a burden; it was liberating. It gave me a sense of control over my new life. By prioritizing my studies and cutting out distractions—no TV, minimal social media, fewer outings—I found enough hours in the day to excel in school, work enough to pay bills, and still get six hours of sleep to recharge. **Productivity became my new adrenaline.** And as the semesters rolled by, that discipline paid off: I aced my exams, earned scholarships, and built a reputation as one of the most driven students in the program.

I still remember the day Professor Jenkins pulled me aside after anatomy class. "Mark," he said, eyeing me with curiosity, "I've been teaching for twenty years, and I've never seen anyone attack their studies with your intensity. What drives you?"

I hesitated, unsure whether to reveal my past. Then I decided on honesty—the truth would eventually come out anyway. "I spent five years in prison," I told him quietly. "I'm making up for lost time."

Instead of judgment, I saw respect in his eyes. "Well," he replied, "if all my students had your hunger for education, I'd never have to curve a grade again." That moment stayed with me—the first time I realized my background could be transformed from a liability into evidence of my determination.

Discipline Doctrine: "Discipline is the bridge between your current reality and your distant dreams. Build that bridge daily through consistent habits, and you'll cross terrain others claim is impassable."

Two years later, I earned my **Degree in Respiratory Therapy**, then passed the board exams to become a Respiratory Therapist. On graduation day, as I walked across the stage in my cap and gown, I felt an overwhelming surge of emotion. Just a few years prior I had been wearing a prison uniform, identified by a number. Now I stood in front of a crowd wearing a graduation robe, my name printed in the program with an academic honor by it.

I'll never forget the moment I held my diploma in hand—I actually closed my eyes and silently said *thank you* for the second chance to reinvent myself. It wasn't just a piece of paper; it was proof that I could transform my life through effort and learning. But I also knew this was only the beginning. Like climbing one peak only to see a higher summit beyond, my success in respiratory therapy school revealed a deeper truth: **I loved learning and pushing my limits**, and I wasn't going to stop here.

The Power of Continuous Growth

True to that feeling, I continued to expand my education. Over the next few years I completed a Bachelor's in Nursing while working full-time at a hospital and two nursing homes over 60 hours a week. I chose extra rotations in the ER and ICU, intrigued by the complexity of helping patients breathe. That curiosity led me to pursue a specialized degree in **nursing as a Nurse Anesthetist** next.

Co-workers wondered why I'd subject myself to more schooling when I already had a solid career. But I was driven by an insatiable hunger to grow. I remembered the Stoic maxim, *"As long as you live, keep learning how to live."* To me, *lifelong learning* wasn't just a cliché—it was the very strategy that had lifted me from rock bottom.

Every new skill or qualification was another tool in my toolbox, another way to serve and succeed. So, I attended nursing classes at night while saving money from my nursing job. It was a grueling period—twelve-hour hospital shifts followed by three-hour lectures—but I felt alive and purposeful. Where once I might have complained, now I embraced the challenge. I had chosen this path, after all, and that sense of ownership over my life made even the hard days meaningful.

The power of this multi-disciplinary approach became clear to me one night in the hospital. I was working a late shift when a critical patient's ventilator malfunctioned. While the technical team was still 20 minutes away, I used my unique combination of respiratory therapy knowledge and emerging computer science understanding to diagnose the issue and implement a temporary fix. The attending physician later commented, "I've never seen someone bridge two completely different fields like that in a crisis."

That moment crystallized something I now consider essential entrepreneurial wisdom: **The most innovative solutions often emerge at the intersection of different disciplines.** The white space between established fields is fertile ground for new ideas. Steve Jobs understood this when he combined calligraphy aesthetics with computer design. Elon Musk applies physics principles to business challenges. In your own journey, don't view your diverse experiences as disconnected—see them as unique puzzle pieces that, when combined, create a picture no one else can replicate.

Convergence Concept: "Your unique value doesn't come from mastering one narrow skill—it emerges when you connect seemingly unrelated domains. The wider your knowledge spans, the more original your insights become."

By my late-twenties, armed with dual degrees in nursing and respiratory therapy, I found myself in a place I could hardly have imagined a decade earlier. I had a rewarding career healing patients and a stable life. But my youthful dream of building a business had not faded—in fact, with each accomplishment, that dream burned brighter.

Working in healthcare, I constantly spotted problems in need of solutions: patients confused about their medications, clinics juggling inefficient paper records, understaffed hospitals struggling to schedule nurses. I began jotting down ideas for services and products to solve these issues. One idea in particular grabbed me: a software platform to help hospitals optimize their nurse scheduling and patient education. It combined my medical knowledge with technology—an arena I was fascinated by but had limited formal experience in. The more I thought about it, the more it excited me. Yet, I knew I lacked the tech skills to bring it to life. *No matter*, I thought—I could learn those too.

The Courage to Begin Again

So, at 28, I embarked on earning a **degree in Computer Science**. Some of my friends and colleagues thought I was **crazy**—why not just enjoy the fruits of my hard work instead of starting over again in a whole new field? But I believed in **constant reinvention**. I often recalled Elon Musk's observation, *"I think it is possible for ordinary people to choose to be extraordinary."* I considered myself an ordinary guy—I had no special advantages, I had stumbled and fallen hard—but I had **extraordinary goals**.

I chose to chase a vision of myself that exceeded what anyone (including my old self) thought possible. And if that meant being a student yet again, so be it. At night, after long hospital shifts, I would fire up my second-hand laptop and immerse myself in online programming courses. I learned to code from scratch, building simple websites at first and eventually more complex applications. Every new concept mastered was like adding a fresh color to my palette, allowing me to paint the entrepreneurial vision I dreamed of.

Learning computer science was humbling—there were moments I felt totally out of my depth, stuck on a piece of code at 2 AM with bleary eyes and a pounding head. But each time I hit a wall, I thought back to all the obstacles I'd overcome before. This was just another puzzle to solve, another test of perseverance. I applied the same strategy I'd honed years ago: break the big problem into smaller pieces, tackle them one by one, and never be too proud to ask for help or look up answers.

Slowly but surely, I became proficient in coding and software design. Perhaps the most satisfying project was building the prototype for that nurse-scheduling app I'd envisioned. I spent countless weekends developing it in my living room, fueled by black coffee and sheer determination. There were plenty of bugs and iterations, but eventually it started to work. I could hardly contain my excitement the first time I demo'd it successfully at a small medical professionals' meetup. Here I was, an ex-prisoner turned nurse turned programmer, showing a tech solution I created to solve a real-world healthcare problem. It was a surreal and proud moment.

Reinvention Rule: "Never allow your past to dictate your future, but always let it inform your wisdom. Your unique path—especially the difficult parts—contains the seeds of your greatest competitive advantage."

From Side Project to Startup

Encouraged by positive feedback, I officially launched my first business—a startup offering the scheduling software—and dove headlong into the world of entrepreneurship. The first year was anything but smooth. I pitched my product to dozens of hospital administrators and clinic owners. Most slammed the door in my face or were polite enough to say "interesting idea" but never called back. I burned through my modest savings to keep the project afloat, and there were nights I wondered if I was just fooling myself.

During those times, I took comfort in stories of entrepreneurs who had struggled before succeeding. I remembered Colonel Sanders being rejected over a thousand times before franchising KFC, and Sylvester Stallone's refusal to sell the *Rocky* script without getting a chance to star in it. These examples reminded me that **perseverance** separates those who merely dream from those who **do**.

I adopted a simple rule: *no matter how many no's I get, I only need one yes to change the game.* Whenever I felt like quitting, I'd repeat to myself, *"Persistence is very important. You should not give up unless you are forced to give up,"* as Elon Musk famously said. And I wasn't being forced to give up—the only one who could stop me was *me*, and I wasn't about to sabotage my own dream.

I remember one particularly harsh rejection from the head of a major hospital network. After my presentation, she listed a dozen reasons why my software wouldn't work in their environment. As I packed up my laptop, feeling deflated, she added, "Besides, what makes you think someone like you understands our problems?" The implicit judgment in her tone was clear. For a moment, I felt that old shame rising—was my background still defining me?

That evening, instead of giving in to discouragement, I did something different. I mapped out each of her twelve objections and systematically addressed them, improving my software with each fix. Her unconscious bias had inadvertently given me a roadmap for making my product better. Three months later, I approached a competing hospital group with the improved version. The CEO was impressed enough to sign a pilot contract, and later told me it was my unique perspective as both a healthcare worker and technologist that made the difference—the very diversity of experience that set me apart.

This taught me an invaluable lesson: **sometimes your greatest perceived weaknesses become your most distinctive strengths**. What others see as disadvantages—an unconventional background, experience across multiple fields rather than deep expertise in one—can become your most powerful differentiators in the market.

Bit by bit, progress came. A small clinic decided to pilot my software—and they loved it. With that testimonial, I convinced a second client to sign on. I'll never forget the day I secured my first major contract with a regional hospital system. After the administrator shook my hand and said, "We'll give it a try," I walked out to my car and cried tears of joy. Not because of the money (though that was important to keep the business going), but because of what it represented: **validation**.

It validated that I could see an idea through from conception to reality. It proved that my past was not a permanent anchor dragging me down—in fact, it was now *fuel* propelling me upward, giving me the grit to handle the highs and lows of startup life. That year, my little company grew to a small team of five employees (including two other ex-inmates I happily hired, knowing the value of a second chance). We continued to improve the product and expand to new clients. My journey from prison to proprietor had come full circle in the most literal way: I had gone from being a ward of the state to partnering with state hospitals as a business owner. Life has a poetic way of rewarding those who persist.

Persistence Principle: "When faced with rejection, don't just persist—evolve. Each 'no' is data for refining your approach. The path to success isn't a straight line but a series of intelligent pivots based on feedback."

The Value of Transformation

I consulted with two talented web developers who had been running their agency as a general partnership for three years. When I asked about their partnership agreement, they exchanged uncomfortable glances—they had nothing in writing. Everything had been based on a handshake and their friendship.

Their business was generating over $300,000 annually, yet either partner could make decisions that legally bound both of them. Even more concerning, if one partner made a costly mistake with a client project, both their personal assets were on the line.

I asked them to consider a scenario: "What if one of you decides to leave the business? Who keeps the clients? How do you value the company? What if one of you becomes disabled?" Their silence confirmed they hadn't considered these questions.

Within two months, they had formed an LLC with a comprehensive operating agreement that addressed ownership percentages, decision-making authority, dispute resolution processes, and exit strategies. The transformation wasn't just legal—it was psychological. With clear boundaries established, their friendship actually strengthened, and they approached client work with renewed confidence.

This story illustrates a critical truth: proper structure isn't just about legal protection—it's about creating clarity that allows relationships and businesses to thrive.

My client Rachel provides a perfect illustration of the S-Corporation's power. She ran a successful marketing consultancy as a single-member LLC for three years, consistently earning around $250,000 annually. As her default LLC tax treatment had her paying self-employment tax on the entire amount, her tax burden was substantial.

After analyzing her finances, I recommended electing S-Corporation status. We determined $125,000 would be a reasonable salary for her role based on industry standards. After making the election, she still paid full employment taxes on her $125,000 salary, but the remaining $125,000 in profit could be taken as distributions free from self-employment tax.

The result? She saved approximately $19,125 in self-employment taxes the very first year (15.3% of $125,000). Yes, she incurred some new expenses—payroll processing fees, additional accounting costs, and more paperwork—but these totaled less than $3,000 annually, leaving her with over $16,000 in net tax savings.

What did Rachel do with this newfound capital? She invested it back into her business, hiring her first employee and expanding her client base. By year five, her business had tripled in size. The S-Corporation election hadn't just saved her money—it had provided the financial breathing room to pursue strategic growth.

This example demonstrates why structure isn't merely a technical decision—it can be the difference between steady success and explosive growth.

Standing in my office one evening long after my team had left, I looked at the framed degrees on my wall—Nursing, Respiratory Therapy, Computer Science—and at the logo of my company on the door. In that quiet moment, I understood a truth deeper than any diploma or bank balance could convey: **education and entrepreneurship had not only altered my path, they had transformed me**.

The greatest reward of this journey wasn't the credentials or the contracts; it was the person I had become through the process. I thought back to Jim Rohn's insight: *"The major value in life is not what you get. The major value in life is what you become."* By striving to expand my mind, by overcoming trials and never settling, I had *become* a man of resilience, vision, and compassion. I had reinvented myself completely, and in doing so, discovered my potential was far greater than I'd ever dreamed.

Now, as a budding entrepreneur, I continue to learn **every single day**. I wake up each morning excited to devour new knowledge—whether it's a book on leadership, a podcast on business strategy, or a lesson from a mistake we made last week. I've made it a habit to remain a student of life, permanently. After all, **reinvention is not a one-time event, but a way of living**.

My story proves that it doesn't matter where you start or how many detours you take; what matters is the relentless commitment to growth. If I can go from a prison cell to building businesses, then *truly, anything is possible.* And that is the message I want every aspiring entrepreneur to remember: **you are not defined by your past, but by the actions you choose to take today**. Every experience, good or bad, can be alchemized into growth. Every skill you learn becomes a rung on the ladder to your dreams. All it really takes is embracing the mindset of constant improvement and having the courage to climb, one step at a time.

Key Takeaways (Chapter 2)

- **Design Your Destiny:** Don't drift—chart a clear plan for your life and goals. Taking the time to set a direction (education, career, business) will give you a mission to strive for and protect you from outside distractions.

- **Never Stop Learning:** Commit to being a lifelong learner. Whether through formal education or self-education, keep expanding your skills and knowledge. Remember, *"Formal education will make you a living; self-education will make you a fortune."* Make daily learning a habit to continually increase your value and opportunities.

- **Master Time Management:** Treat time as your most precious asset. Plan your days (use calendars, time blocks, to-do lists) so that your hours align with your goals. As Jim Rohn said, either you control your day or it controls you—so take charge of each day's schedule to steadily build your dream.

- **Be Relentlessly Resourceful:** Lack of money, connections, or experience is not an excuse to quit—it's a challenge to get creative. Use what you have at hand and turn constraints into advantages. Can't afford a solution? Teach yourself new skills or find an alternative route. **Entrepreneurs make the most of what they have**; they find a way through, around, or over any obstacle.

- **Persevere Through Setbacks:** Every venture will encounter failures, from failed exams to rejected business pitches. Expect them, and resolve to learn and adapt each time. Perseverance is the great equalizer—if you stay in the game and keep improving, you'll eventually find the breakthrough. As the saying goes, a winner is just a loser who tried one more time. Keep trying *one more time*, every time, and you'll be amazed at what you can achieve.

- **Find Your Intersection of Skills:** Your most valuable contributions often emerge at the crossroads of your diverse experiences. Don't view your varied background as unfocused—it's the unique combination of skills that no one else possesses.

With the foundation of personal transformation and education firmly established, it's time to explore how to turn promising ideas into tangible realities. In Chapter 3, we'll delve into the art and science of bringing concepts to life—and the crucial difference between dreamers who imagine what could be and founders who create what will be.

3

_–·–_

FROM DREAM TO REALITY

I sat at my kitchen table at 2 AM, a blank business plan template glaring from my laptop screen and a dozen half-formed ideas scribbled in my journal. Just a week earlier I had boldly pivoted my career (as you read in Chapter 2), full of enthusiasm about building something of my own. Now, in the quiet hush of the night, I felt that enthusiasm waver. I had plenty of dreams—**too many, in fact**—but analysis-paralysis had me in its grip. Each idea seemed to sparkle in theory, yet I was terrified to choose one and make a move. What if I picked the wrong idea? What if I failed and looked foolish after leaving my safe career?

Creation Catalyst: "Ideas are like seeds in your pocket—valuable only when planted. Plant many, nurture the strongest, and accept that some will wither while others bloom beyond your imagination."

The Idea Graveyard

One of those ideas in my journal had been gnawing at me for months. It was a concept for a passion project I was _sure_ could make an impact. I had talked about it endlessly to my friends, sketched logos and slogans in the margins of my notebook, and even fantasized about how I'd pitch it on a big stage. But that night, I faced a hard truth: in spite of all my dreaming, I hadn't taken a single concrete step toward making it happen. The idea was alive only in my head. **That realization stung.** I closed my journal, frustrated with myself. Before heading to bed, I jotted in big letters on a sticky note: *"An idea in your head has zero value until you try to make it real."* I needed to see that first thing in the morning.

As fate would have it, the universe delivered a wake-up call sooner than expected. The very next day, while scrolling through news on my phone, I froze—a startup was launching a project eerily similar to my beloved idea. Someone else out there had not only dreamed up the same concept, but they were actually doing it! My heart pounded. At first I felt a pang of envy (and frankly, self-pity). *That could have been me in the article*, I thought, if only I'd had the courage to move faster. But envy quickly gave way to inspiration.

Here was proof that the idea *could* work in the real world—and the only difference between that founder and me was that they took action while I had only been *thinking* about it.

In that moment, I made a promise to myself: **I would never again let hesitation turn my dreams into "what-ifs."** It was time to transform from a serial dreamer into a doer. I realized that no one was going to show up and hand me permission to start—I had to give myself that permission. My perspective shifted from fearing failure to fearing regret. I'd rather *try and stumble* than keep watching from the sidelines as others brought *my* ideas to life.

That week, I took my first concrete steps. They weren't perfect or earth-shattering—a rough outline, a simple prototype, a couple of cold emails—but they felt empowering. Each small action whispered to me: *"See? This is how a dream starts to become real."*

The Power of an Idea (and Why Execution Matters)

That experience taught me something profound: **ideas are powerful, but execution is what gives them power**. You can have the most revolutionary idea in the world, but if it stays locked in your mind or scribbled on napkins, it might as well not exist. I'm not alone in learning this. The entrepreneurial world is full of brilliant minds who emphasize doing over just dreaming. As legendary automaker Henry Ford famously put it, *"Vision without execution is just hal lucination."* An idea by itself is like a beautiful blueprint—inspiring, yes, but it won't shelter anyone until someone lays the bricks.

Execution Excellence: "The gap between dreamers and builders isn't talent or luck—it's the willingness to endure the messy middle where ideas collide with reality. Embrace that messy middle; it's where all great ventures are truly born."

I used to fall in love with my ideas and guard them closely, thinking that just having a great concept was enough. But I eventually understood a key truth: **the value of an idea is zero until you act on it**. Thomas Edison—one of the most prolific inventors in history—respected doers over ideators. *"I have more respect for the fellow with a single idea who gets there than for the fellow with a thousand ideas who does nothing,"* Edison said decades ago. When I first came across that quote, it hit me like a lightning bolt. I was that fellow with a thousand ideas bouncing around in my head and notebooks. Edison's words made me ask: what's the use of a thousand ideas if none ever see the light of day?

I remember the morning after discovering that startup had launched "my" idea. Instead of wallowing in disappointment, I decided to test another concept I'd been nurturing—a mobile application that would help hospital patients track their medication schedules and recovery milestones. Unlike my previous patterns of endless planning, I gave myself a 48-hour deadline to create something tangible.

What happened next taught me an invaluable lesson about momentum. I sketched wireframes, researched technical requirements, and even interviewed three nurses about the concept—all within that narrow window. The prototype was crude—literally paper sketches I had photographed and linked together in a presentation—but it was *real*. When I showed it to a physician friend for feedback, she didn't just offer suggestions; she immediately introduced me to the hospital's innovation director who wanted to discuss a pilot program.

That single act of creating something physical, something others could see and touch, generated more opportunity in two days than all my previous months of "thinking about it." I learned that execution creates its own gravity—pulling in resources, connections, and opportunities that remain invisible to those who merely contemplate.

The difference between people who dream and those who *do* often comes down to a simple habit: taking the first step. It's normal to romanticize the "Eureka!" moment when an idea is born. We've all heard stories of geniuses who came up with a brilliant idea in a flash of inspiration. But those stories can be misleading if we forget what happens next. The hard work *after* the lightbulb moment is what actually brings an idea to life. In fact, Edison himself, who literally invented the lightbulb, famously remarked that *"genius is one percent inspiration, ninety-nine percent perspiration"*. That couldn't be more true in entrepreneurship. Brainstorming an idea is that 1%—the spark. The other 99% is the sweat: writing the code, crafting the business plan, calling potential customers, refining the product.

My late-night soul-searching made it clear that I had to stop worshipping ideas for their own sake and start executing them, flaws and all. I turned one of my journal pages into a mantra in bold letters: *"Action turns imagination into reality."* It was a reminder to myself that no matter how vivid my vision, it would remain a hallucination (thank you Mr. Ford) unless I *did something* about it.

Iteration Over Perfection: Every Big Success Started Small

Once I started taking action on my idea, I quickly confronted another challenge: my first attempts were, to put it kindly, rough. I had a vision of how amazing my business could be, and what I had in front of me was *not* that. It's tempting at that point to get discouraged or to stall, waiting until everything is "perfect" before you put your work out into the world. But here's another lesson from seasoned creators and builders: **embrace iteration and imperfection; it's the only path to excellence.** Every major success you see out there—every bestselling book or billion-dollar startup—began as an early draft, a prototype, a *version 1.0* that would probably make its creators cringe today. And that is completely normal.

Iteration Insight: "Perfection isn't achieved through perfect first attempts but through relentless refinement. The masters aren't those who avoid mistakes—they're the ones who transform mistakes into stepping stones faster than everyone else."

Consider the story of J.K. Rowling. Her fantastical idea of a young wizard came to her spontaneously during a train ride. Caught without a proper notebook, she famously jotted down the initial concept of *Harry Potter* on whatever scrap of paper she could find—reportedly a napkin on that train. That scrap of an idea was the seed of a global phenomenon. But the Harry Potter we know was not born overnight. Rowling spent years developing the story, writing and rewriting. The manuscript for the first book was rejected by 12 different publishers before one gave it a chance.

Imagine if she had given up after the first rejection, or decided that her idea wasn't "perfect" enough to share with the world. We'd have lost an entire universe of stories. Rowling's journey underscores that **the first version of your idea is just the beginning**. You must be willing to improve it, bit by bit. As she later reflected, every rejection letter only fueled her determination to prove her story's worth.

Thomas Edison's journey to inventing the lightbulb is another classic example of iteration in action. We often remember the lightbulb as a brilliant *idea*, but it was the relentless trial-and-error process that made it a reality. Edison and his team tested *thousands* of different materials for the filament before finally finding one that worked. In fact, Edison joked, *"I have not failed. I've just found 10,000 ways that won't work"*.

That quip is more than just humor; it's a blueprint for innovation. Each "failed" attempt wasn't really a failure at all—it was a step forward, a lesson in what **not** to do, bringing him closer to a solution. This mindset—treating each setback or iteration as part of the process—is gold for an entrepreneur. It teaches you to view prototypes, tests, and even flops as invaluable data rather than proof that your idea is bad.

I experienced this firsthand with my own healthcare scheduling software. My first prototype crashed during a live demonstration to a room full of nursing administrators. While my face burned with embarrassment, I forced myself to stay present and take notes on exactly what failed and why. That evening, I didn't just fix the bug—I completely redesigned the user interface based on questions the nurses had asked during the demonstration.

Three weeks later, I returned with version 2.0. The improvement was so dramatic that the same department head who had seemed disinterested initially now wanted to know when she could implement it. What she didn't realize was that her original confusion and the system's failure had been the exact catalyst needed to create something truly useful. That moment taught me that **sometimes your product needs to break publicly before it can become unbreakable**.

In my own journey, I had to learn to get comfortable with *beta versions*—of my product, of my marketing strategy, even of myself as a founder. My first workshop attracted only a handful of customers and my initial website was laughably simple. But you know what? Those early versions existed, whereas my "perfect" plans did not. I could gather feedback from real users, refine the next iteration, and get better each time. I adopted the mantra: *"Done is better than perfect, because done can be improved."* Every draft business plan, every demo, every pitch that didn't land taught me something. Over time, I started to see "failure" differently—not as a verdict on my idea, but as a necessary step in shaping it. This echoes a famous insight from the Stoic philosopher Marcus Aurelius: *"The impediment to action advances action. What stands in the way becomes the way.".* The obstacles in developing your idea (the glitches, the rejections, the slow sales at first) are not signs to quit; they are the way *forward*, guiding you on how to tweak and improve.

Let go of the illusion that your idea must emerge fully formed and flawless. Elizabeth Gilbert, in her book *Big Magic*, warns that perfectionism is just fear in high heels—it masquerades as a high standard, but really it just prevents you from finishing anything. She advises creatives to give themselves permission to be imperfect, because that's the only way the magic gets out. I eventually embraced this advice. Instead of aiming for **perfection**, I aimed for **progress**. I created a motto for our team: *"Version 1.0 is supposed to be your worst—celebrate it, then make Version 1.1 a little better."* When you take that approach, you free yourself to actually start. You begin to see your business idea as a living thing that will evolve through trial, feedback, and persistence.

Progress Path: "The pursuit of perfection paralyzes progress. Launch with what you have, learn from what happens, and build what should be. Your market wants solutions, not flawlessness."

Beyond the Napkin: Practical Tools for Idea Development
Problem-Solution Journaling

One of the most practical techniques I discovered for generating viable business ideas was something I call "Problem-Solution Journaling." Each night before bed, I wrote down three specific problems or frustrations I encountered during the day—no matter how small or seemingly insignificant. They could be as simple as "Couldn't find my keys this morning" or as complex as "Hospital scheduling software crashed during shift change."

The next morning, before checking email or social media, I'd spend ten minutes brainstorming possible solutions to each problem. The key rule: I must generate at least three potential solutions per problem, and at least one solution must be technologically feasible with existing tools.

This simple practice accomplishes several things simultaneously: it trains your mind to spot problems (the seeds of opportunity), it exercises your solution-generating muscles daily, and it creates a growing inventory of potential business ideas rooted in real-world needs. Even better, it ensures you're addressing problems you personally understand and care about—a key foundation for authentic entrepreneurship.

After just one month of this practice, you'll have documented 90 problems and 270 potential solutions. Review this list monthly, and patterns will emerge. You'll start seeing which problems consistently aggravate you (revealing your passions) and which solutions excite you most (revealing your natural interests).

The Vision Board: Picturing Your "Why"

It's easy to get lost in a sea of random ideas. A vision board is a powerful way to anchor yourself to what truly matters to you. Take a moment (yes, right now!) to articulate the core **"why"** behind your entrepreneurial journey. What ultimate goal or lifestyle are you working toward? What values do you want your business to embody?

Find or draw images that represent that vision—the kind of impact you want to have, the freedom you're seeking, the customers you dream of helping. You can do this digitally (e.g. a Pinterest board or a simple document with pasted images) or physically with magazine clippings on a poster. The point is to create a visual reminder of the dream you're aiming to turn into reality.

- **How to do it:** In the center of your board, write a short bold statement of your mission (for example, *"Empower kids to love science through play"* or *"Make healthy eating accessible for busy families"*—whatever fuels you). Around it, cluster pictures or words that resonate with that mission: a snapshot of a person you'd love to help, a product that inspires you, a word cloud of values (freedom, creativity, community, etc.). Let your creative side run wild here—this is personal, so there's no "wrong" way to design your vision board.

- **Use it as a compass:** Hang this vision board somewhere you'll see it often. As you brainstorm and later refine business ideas, refer back to your board. Does an idea excite you when you compare it to the board? Does it align with the "why" you've depicted? Your vision board will help you filter which ideas genuinely light you up and fit your long-term vision. It also keeps you motivated on tough days—it's a snapshot of the destination you're working toward.

Lightning Round: 5 Minutes, 20 Ideas

One of the biggest threats to innovation is overthinking. To blast past that barrier, challenge yourself to an *idea lightning round*. This is all about speed and quantity, not quality. Set a timer for five minutes. Ready... go! In those five minutes, try to write down 20 business ideas. Yes, 20. They can be utterly ridiculous or painfully mundane—it doesn't matter. If you're focused and don't stop writing, you won't have time to judge or censor yourself, which is exactly the point.

1. **Set your timer (5 minutes):** Use your phone or watch. Promise yourself that you won't do anything else until the alarm rings.

2. **Write every idea that pops up:** Don't stop to evaluate. If your brain whispers "open a cat café" or "build an app that plans outfits," just scribble it down. Keep going. The urgency is key—it turns off the part of your brain that says "Is this idea good/bad?" and just forces output.

3. **Aim for twenty:** If you hit 20 ideas before five minutes, awesome—keep going! If you hit the time limit with fewer, no worries—maybe extend to 7 or 10 minutes next time. The goal is to push past your comfort zone. Usually the first few ideas will be obvious ones, the next few will be wacky or nonsense (when your brain is saying "Uh oh, I'm out of ideas!"), but if you keep pushing, you might strike a novel idea around number 15 or 18 that surprises you.

4. **Review and refine:** Only after the lightning round ends, look at what you wrote. Circle any ideas that immediately make you sit up and think, "Hmm, there's something here." You might find that among the silly or safe ideas, there's one or two that have real potential or spark joy for you. Even the outrageous ones might contain a nugget you can tweak into a usable concept.

This exercise works because it forces you out of analysis mode and into pure creation mode. It's a favorite of mine whenever I feel stuck or if I notice I'm procrastinating on idea generation due to fear of not coming up with something "good enough." Plus, it's actually fun—you'll likely laugh at some of the wild things you come up with under time pressure. (And who knows, sometimes the world *does* need a cat café or an outfit-planning app!)

Generation Gem: "Quantity breeds quality in ideation. The first five ideas come from your conscious mind; the next ten from your subconscious; only after twenty do you start accessing the truly original corners of your creativity."

The AI Advantage: Brainstorming with Artificial Intelligence

In today's world, we have an amazing brainstorming buddy available 24/7: **AI tools** like ChatGPT. Whenever I feel stuck or I'm searching for fresh angles, I fire up ChatGPT and treat it like a no-judgment idea machine. For example, when I was ideating for a fitness-related business, I typed in a prompt: *"Give me 10 quirky business ideas at the intersection of fitness and education."* Within seconds, I had suggestions—from virtual reality gym classes for kids to a podcast that teaches history while you jog. Not every idea it generated was viable (some were downright wacky), but a couple were intriguing and got my own creative gears turning in new directions.

Tools like ChatGPT can serve as a catalyst. They can't replace your vision or the validation of a real market, but they can certainly help you expand the realm of possibilities. Sometimes an off-the-wall suggestion from the AI will make you think, *"Huh, I hadn't considered that angle."* You might refine or combine that into something original. I've used ChatGPT to brainstorm names for products, to outline potential revenue streams I might have missed, and even to role-play as a potential customer so I can hear "questions" a buyer might ask. It's like having an infinite whiteboard and a brainstorming partner who never runs out of energy. So, when you're brainstorming, **don't brainstorm alone**—bring in friends, mentors, or your friendly neighborhood AI to bounce ideas around.

Brainstorming Breakthrough: "Creativity thrives in collision—between disciplines, between problems and solutions, between your expertise and others' perspectives. The most valuable ideas often emerge when you create intentional collisions."

The key in this phase is to suspend judgment. There will be a time to scrutinize and narrow down your ideas (we'll get to that), but initially, you want to generate a rich pool of inspiration to draw from. Be playful and adventurous. Give yourself permission to be silly or audacious. Often, the breakthrough comes right after a series of silly thoughts—you have to wade through the absurd to get to the profound. Brainstorming is a bit like panning for gold: you sift through a lot of sand to find a nugget. Keep sifting, and don't get discouraged if you haven't struck gold in the first five minutes. The more raw material you create, the higher the chance you'll discover something truly exciting.

Stop Waiting and Start Creating

At this point, you've done some soul-searching, generated a bunch of ideas, and learned the secret that **action is the ingredient that turns imagination into reality**. You've seen how the greats—from authors to inventors—treated ideas as the starting line, not the finish line. You have tools in your kit to help you brainstorm freely and then zero in on what truly matters to you. The only thing left is the most important step of all: *begin*.

I once mentored a brilliant doctor who had developed a revolutionary technique for minimally invasive surgery. For three years, he refined the procedure on paper, creating increasingly detailed diagrams and protocols. "I'll submit it to medical journals once it's perfect," he told me. Meanwhile, patients who could have benefited continued suffering with outdated methods.

After months of urging him to take action, I finally asked him to imagine standing before a patient and explaining why he'd withheld a potentially life-changing innovation. "Would you tell them you were waiting for perfection?" I asked. "Or would you admit you were simply afraid?"

The next week, he scheduled a presentation at his hospital. Six months later, his technique was being implemented in operating rooms across the country. Today, thousands of patients experience less pain and faster recovery because he finally understood that an imperfect solution that exists helps more people than a perfect solution that doesn't.

This story perfectly illustrates a principle I've come to live by: **The world needs your contribution now, not your perfection eventually.**

No more waiting for the perfect moment or the perfect idea. Major businesses and life-changing projects all started as a humble first step. Remember my story at the start of this chapter—I spent ages waiting and worrying, until a dose of reality pushed me to just launch something. Don't wait for life to push you; push yourself. If you have an idea that makes your heart race a little, **pursue it**. If you're unsure which idea to choose, pick one and run a small experiment. You'll soon learn if it's viable or if you should try a different approach. Either way, you are moving forward, turning dreams into tangible projects.

Every day that you take even a small action, you're distancing yourself from the majority of "someday" dreamers and joining the ranks of makers and doers. It's okay if your idea isn't crystal clear yet. It's okay if it changes and morphs as you iterate—in fact, it *should*. The path will reveal itself as you walk it. As you finish this chapter, I challenge you to do one thing **today** related to your ideas: sketch a draft logo, write a paragraph about your concept, email someone in the industry for insights, even use ChatGPT to flesh out a quick business model outline. Just *do something*.

Entrepreneurship is a continual dance between vision and execution. You've got the vision; now take that leap of execution. Trust that you'll learn and adapt just as every successful founder before you has done. Your dream deserves a chance at life outside your head. So get out there and build it. Don't let another day, week, or year slip by. As one popular proverb reminds us, **"The best time to plant a tree was 20 years ago. The second best time is now."** The same goes for your idea. Start planting that seed *now*.

Action Anthem: "Dreams flourish in action, not intention. The universe doesn't reward those who wait for permission—it rewards those who move with conviction despite uncertainty. Your future self will thank you not for what you planned, but for what you built."

Stop waiting and start creating. The world is waiting to see what you'll do with that spark only you have. This is your moment to turn your dream into the next great story of entrepreneurship—and I, for one, can't wait to see it come to life.

As we move into Chapter 4, we'll map the entire entrepreneurial journey from idea to exit. With your concept now beginning to take tangible form, you need to understand the full terrain ahead—the challenges and opportunities at each stage of building a successful venture. This roadmap will help you navigate with confidence, knowing not just where you stand today, but where your path can lead tomorrow.

4

— · —

FROM IDEA TO EXIT — THE ENTREPRENEURIAL JOURNEY

If you've made it this far, congratulations—you've already separated yourself from the countless dreamers who never take the crucial first step. You've learned to break free from limiting beliefs, to continuously develop your skills, and to transform ideas into action. Now let's chart the complete journey that lies ahead—from where you are now to a potential successful exit.

Think of this chapter as your roadmap for the complete entrepreneurial journey. We'll explore each critical stage from early validation to potential exit, highlighting the challenges, strategies, and mindset shifts needed at each phase. This isn't just theoretical—I'll share real experiences from my own ventures and those of other founders I've advised.

Stage 1: Validation — Making Sure Your Idea Has Legs

You've got an idea that excites you—great! But before investing significant time and resources, you need to validate that others share your enthusiasm. This is where many first-time entrepreneurs stumble. They fall so deeply in love with their concept that they skip this crucial validation step, only to build something nobody wants.

The Validation Dilemma

I remember when Alex, a brilliant engineer friend, spent 18 months building what he thought was a revolutionary app for scheduling group activities. He invested his savings, worked nights and weekends, and even mortgaged his house to fund development. When he finally launched, the response was crickets. Why? He had never actually confirmed that his target users—busy parents—would pay for such a solution.

The painful truth is that nearly 42% of startups fail because they build something no one wants. The good news? This fate is entirely avoidable through proper validation.

Validation Methodology: "Before you build the house, make sure someone wants to live in it. Before you write the code, confirm someone will use it. And before you invest your soul, verify others will value it."

Let me walk you through a simple but effective validation process:

1. **Problem Validation**: First, ensure the problem you're solving actually exists and is painful enough that people want a solution. This seems obvious, but you'd be surprised how many founders skip this step. My approach: Conduct at least 20 interviews with potential customers focused solely on understanding their frustrations—not pitching your solution. Ask questions like: "What's the most challenging part of [area your product addresses]?" or "How do you currently solve this issue?" Look for emotional responses and workarounds that indicate genuine pain points.

2. **Solution Validation**: Once you've confirmed the problem exists, test whether your proposed solution resonates. My approach: Create a simple landing page describing your solution with a "pre-order" or "join waitlist" button. Dri-

ve small amounts of targeted traffic to this page (perhaps $100-200 worth of ads). A 2-5% conversion rate suggests interest. For B2B products, try to secure letters of intent from potential customers saying they'd try your product when available.

3. **Pricing Validation**: Finally, determine if people will pay what you need to charge. My approach: While still pre-launch, present different pricing options to potential customers and gauge reactions. Watch faces, not just words—people often say they'd pay but wince at actual numbers. If possible, collect actual pre-orders or deposits to confirm true willingness to pay.

The MVP Breakthrough

For my healthcare scheduling software, validation came when I showed a simple prototype to three hospital administrators who immediately asked, "When can we pilot this?" Their enthusiasm wasn't just encouraging—it was concrete evidence of market need.

But validation doesn't always yield positive results, and that's okay too. When I was exploring an idea for a meal planning app, my initial research revealed that while people loved the concept, their willingness to pay was far below what would make the business viable. That early validation saved me from wasting months building something that would have failed financially.

Remember: validation isn't about seeking approval for your idea; it's about gathering honest feedback to refine or even pivot if necessary. Embrace negative feedback—it's cheaper to change direction early than after you've built an entire product.

Validation Victory: "The goal of validation isn't to prove your idea is perfect—it's to identify where it's imperfect before you've invested too much. Each critique is a gift that strengthens your future success."

Stage 2: Foundation Building — Creating Your Operational Base

Once you've validated your concept, it's time to establish the foundation your business will stand on. This means making critical decisions about legal structure (we'll explore this deeply in Chapter 5), setting up financial systems, and assembling your initial team.

The Legal and Financial Framework

Your early structural decisions have long-term implications. I've seen too many founders rush through this stage, creating headaches they could have avoided with proper planning. For example, a friend launched a promising tech company but chose the wrong corporate structure. Three years and significant growth later, when acquisition interest emerged, the company had to undergo a costly and complicated restructuring that nearly tanked the deal.

At minimum, your foundation must include:

1. **Business entity formation**: Choose the right structure (sole proprietorship, LLC, corporation) based on your growth plans, liability concerns, and tax implications. We'll explore this in depth in Chapter 5.

2. **Accounting infrastructure**: Set up proper financial tracking from day one. QuickBooks or Xero are good starting points for most businesses. Establish separate business banking to avoid commingling personal and business finances.

3. **Initial IP protection**: If your idea involves intellectual property, ensure basic protections through trademarks, provisional patents, or copyright registrations as appropriate.

4. **Operating agreements**: If you have co-founders, create clear agreements about equity split, roles and responsibilities, and—critically—what happens if someone wants to leave.

The First Team: Choose Wisely

Your early team members shape your company's future more profoundly than you might realize. This isn't just about skills; it's about shared values and complementary strengths.

When I was building my healthcare software company, my first hire wasn't a developer (though we desperately needed coding help). Instead, I brought on someone who deeply understood hospital workflows and could translate between the technical and medical worlds. This decision proved invaluable—she identified critical features and prevented functionality mistakes that technical expertise alone would have missed.

Team Truth: "Your first five team members will determine your culture, pace, and ultimately your success. Choose people who elevate not just what you build, but how you build it."

Consider both the skills gap your team needs to fill and the culture you want to create. In the early stages, generalists who can wear multiple hats often provide more value than specialists. Look for people who:

- Demonstrate resourcefulness and problem-solving ability

- Share your passion for the mission, not just the potential payday

- Bring complementary skills to balance the founding team

- Can thrive in the uncertainty and rapid change of startup life

Remember that early team members usually accept below-market compensation in exchange for equity or the opportunity to shape something from the ground up. Make sure they understand this trade-off and are genuinely excited about the journey, not just the destination.

Stage 3: Building and Iteration — Creating Your Product

With validation confirming your direction and your foundation in place, now comes the exciting part: actually building your product or service. This stage is where your vision starts becoming tangible, but it's also where many founders get trapped in the pursuit of perfection.

The MVP Mindset

The concept of a Minimum Viable Product (MVP) has become standard startup wisdom for good reason. An MVP is not about creating something cheap or low-quality—it's about identifying the core value you're offering and delivering that with minimal extras.

When we were developing our healthcare scheduling software, our MVP focused on just one function: matching available nurses to open shifts based on qualifications. We excluded dozens of features we "knew" would be useful—reporting, analytics, credential tracking, payroll integration. This restraint wasn't easy, but it allowed us to get real users on the platform within three months instead of a year.

The feedback from those early users shaped our development roadmap more effectively than any amount of internal planning could have. Features we thought would be essential turned out to be unnecessary, while capabilities we hadn't prioritized became development priorities based on user requests.

Iteration Intelligence: "Your first version should solve one problem exceptionally well, not ten problems adequately. Excellence in a narrow focus earns you the right to expand your scope."

Here's my practical approach to MVP development:

1. **List all possible features**: Start by documenting everything you think your product could include.

2. **Ruthlessly prioritize**: Ask of each feature, "Can the product deliver core value without this?" If yes, move it to version 2.0.

3. **Set a launch deadline**: Without a firm date, feature creep is inevitable. I recommend setting an aggressive timeline that makes you slightly uncomfortable.

4. **Establish feedback channels**: Before you launch, create mechanisms to collect user input—surveys, analytics, direct interviews.

5. **Plan your first iteration cycle**: Determine how quickly you'll incorporate feedback into your next version. For software products, I recommend 2-4 week cycles.

Remember, your MVP isn't just about the product—it's about learning. Each interaction with customers provides data that guides your next steps. The faster you can cycle through build-measure-learn loops, the quicker you'll reach product-market fit.

The Technical Debt Trap

One warning about rapid MVP development: beware of accumulating excessive technical debt. Technical debt refers to the future work created when choosing quick solutions over better approaches that would take longer.

I've seen startups crippled by technical decisions made during their MVP phase. One founder I mentored built his platform on a tech stack that was easy to implement but couldn't scale. When success came, his team spent months rebuilding the entire system while competitors raced ahead.

The lesson? Even in your MVP, certain foundational elements deserve careful consideration. Distinguish between features you can add later (good candidates for deferral) and architectural decisions that would be extremely costly to change (worth getting right early).

Stage 4: Traction and Growth — Finding Your Market Foothold

With your MVP in users' hands, the focus shifts to gaining traction—consistently growing your user base and revenue. This is where the rubber meets the road, separating promising concepts from viable businesses.

Finding Your Growth Levers

Each business has specific metrics that drive growth—these are your growth levers. Identifying and optimizing these levers is the difference between struggling and thriving.

For my healthcare staffing platform, our two key growth levers were:

1. Number of nurses who completed at least three shifts through our system

2. Percentage of open hospital shifts filled within 24 hours

We discovered that when we optimized for these metrics specifically—rather than generic goals like "more users" or "more hospitals"—our business grew predictably. When a nurse completed three shifts, they typically became regular users, and when hospitals saw high fill rates, they expanded their use of our platform.

Growth Guidance: "The successful founder focuses not on growth in general, but on the 2-3 specific metrics that drive everything else. Find your unique growth levers and pull them relentlessly."

To identify your growth levers:

1. **Track everything**: In the early stages, measure as many metrics as possible to identify patterns.

2. **Look for correlation with revenue**: Which metrics seem to predict revenue growth most consistently?

3. **Test deliberately**: Run small experiments focused on improving suspected growth levers to confirm their impact.

4. **Double down on what works**: Once you've identified your key levers, allocate resources accordingly.

The Growth Systems Approach

Once you know your growth levers, you need systems to pull them consistently. Ad hoc efforts produce ad hoc results. Systems produce scalable growth.

When my team identified nurse completion rate as our key lever, we built a comprehensive onboarding system: automated reminders before first shifts, check-in texts on shift day, celebration messages after completion, and incentives for completing three shifts within two weeks. This systematic approach tripled our nurse retention compared to our previous informal efforts.

Systems Supremacy: "Build systems that make your key metrics inevitable, not incidental. The founder who relies on inspiration and effort will be outperformed by the founder who creates machines that deliver results regardless of daily motivation."

As you design growth systems, remember they should:

- Function without constant attention from founders

- Produce measurable outcomes linked to growth levers

- Include feedback mechanisms for continuous improvement

- Scale without proportional increases in resources

The beautiful thing about well-designed systems is that they free you from constantly fighting fires, allowing you to focus on strategic opportunities and the next phase of growth.

Stage 5: Scaling — Taking Your Success to New Heights

When you've found product-market fit and established reliable growth systems, you'll face a new challenge: scaling your success. Scaling isn't simply doing more of the same—it requires fundamental evolutions in how your business operates.

The Scaling Inflection Points

In my experience, most businesses encounter predictable inflection points that require structural changes:

1. **Team inflection (typically 10-15 people)**: You can no longer know everything happening in the business or make every decision. You need defined roles, communication processes, and delegation systems.

2. **Management inflection (typically 25-50 people)**: You need a layer of management between founders and front-line employees. This requires promoting individual contributors to leadership roles or hiring experienced managers.

3. **Systems inflection (varies by business model)**: Your scrappy, manual processes no longer support your volume. You need robust systems, often requiring significant investment in technology and process redesign.

4. **Culture inflection (ongoing)**: As you add people who didn't experience your early days, maintaining your core

values requires deliberate effort. Culture must be codified, communicated, and reinforced.

Each inflection point presents both crisis and opportunity. Navigate them successfully, and your company emerges stronger. Fail to adapt, and growth can actually break your business.

Scaling Story: When we hit 30 employees at my healthcare staffing company, I experienced my first true scaling crisis. Tasks were falling through cracks, team members were confused about priorities, and our once-nimble decision making had become painfully slow.

After a particularly frustrating week where we missed a major client deadline, I realized I was the bottleneck. Though it felt counterintuitive, I needed to do less, not more. I restructured our organization into three clear departments, empowered leaders to make decisions without my approval, and implemented weekly metrics reviews instead of daily involvement.

The first month was terrifying—I felt disconnected and worried everything would fall apart without my hands-on approach. Instead, our efficiency improved dramatically. Not only did our performance metrics climb, but team satisfaction increased as people gained ownership over their work.

The Scaling Paradox: "To scale successfully, founders must do less of what made them successful initially. The skills that built your company to 10 people will actually prevent it from growing to 100."

Here are my principles for successful scaling:

1. **Document before you delegate**: Create clear processes for key functions before handing them off.

2. **Hire ahead of the pain**: By the time you desperately need a role filled, you're already behind.

3. **Focus on systems, not solutions**: Instead of solving individual problems, build systems that prevent entire categories of problems.

4. **Maintain decision velocity**: As you grow, fight bureaucracy by establishing clear decision-making frameworks that empower teams.

5. **Preserve your cultural cornerstones**: Identify 3-5 non-negotiable values and reinforce them relentlessly through hiring, recognition, and daily practices.

Scaling is where many founders struggle the most. The entrepreneurial mindset that thrives on chaos and direct control must evolve into leadership that creates order and empowers others. This transformation isn't easy, but it's essential for your company to reach its full potential.

5

—.·—

BUILDING YOUR BUSINESS ARMOR — CHOOSING THE RIGHT LEGAL STRUCTURE

The Founder's Early Crossroads

Evelyn sat at her kitchen table, a half-empty coffee mug beside her business plan. Her startup, a fitness app, was ready to launch — but one big decision loomed. *Do I just start as myself? Form an LLC? A corporation?* She recalled her friend who'd lost everything when a customer lawsuit hit his personal finances — all because he hadn't set up a proper company. Evelyn didn't want to make the same mistake.

Late that night, she phoned her mentor. "Think of a business's legal structure like **armor**," her mentor said. "It's protection and a statement of intent. Choose the right armor for the journey ahead."

That advice stuck. As the sun rose, Evelyn felt the weight lift — she was ready to pick the structure that would shield her dream. Little did she know, this early choice would shape her startup's future in ways she couldn't yet imagine.

Why the Right Structure Matters

Choosing a legal structure isn't just paperwork — it's a foundational decision that affects **liability protection, taxes, scalability, and credibility**. In simple terms, it determines *how much personal* *protection you have, how you and your business are taxed, how easy it is to expand or take on investors,* and even *how professional your business appears* to banks and partners.

As entrepreneur Sara Blakely once said, *"Don't be intimidated by what you don't know. That can be your greatest strength."* In other words, *don't shy away from this decision just because it's unfamiliar.* Embrace it as an empowering step. The right structure early on is part of **building a solid foundation** — one that can save you headaches and heartaches down the road. Think of it like laying the groundwork for a house: a strong foundation makes everything you build on top sturdier.

The Entrepreneur's Armory: U.S. Legal Structures

When it comes to business armor, founders in the U.S. have several options. Each comes with a different level of protection and complexity. Let's explore the main types — from the lightest helmet to the heaviest tank — and see how they stack up:

Sole Proprietorship — The Minimal Gear (Bike Helmet)

Imagine riding into battle with just a bicycle helmet — that's a **sole proprietorship**. It's the default, simplest structure: just you, doing business as *you*. There's no separate legal entity; you don't even file any special paperwork to create one. This is like Evelyn selling her fitness coaching services under her own name with no formal company.

The upside? Full control and ultra simplicity — no formation costs, no separate tax filing (profits are simply *your* income). It's you at your most agile. The **downside is protection — or lack thereof**. In a sole prop, there's **no legal separation between you and the business**. If the business can't pay a debt or gets sued, your personal assets (car, house, savings) are on the line.

In our armor analogy, that helmet might save you from a small knock, but your body (and bank account) is exposed. Sole proprietorships make sense for **low-risk, small-scale startups or side hustles** where you're just testing an idea. The moment you sense real risk — say you sign a significant client contract or see business picking up — it's usually time to **upgrade your armor**. As the saying goes, don't wait for rain to buy an umbrella. In business terms: don't wait for a lawsuit to form an LLC.

General Partnership — Two People, One Helmet

Now picture two riders on a tandem bicycle, sharing one helmet between them — scary, right? That's essentially a **general partnership**. If you and a friend start a business without any formal entity, by default you're a general partnership. It's like a multi-person sole proprietorship.

Easy to start? Absolutely. But the liability is multiplied: **each partner is personally liable for the business — and for each other's decisions**. If your partner incurs a debt or makes a legal mistake, creditors can come after *both* of you, even if you weren't personally involved. In other words, "all for one and one for all" in the worst way.

On the bright side, partnerships enjoy pass-through taxation (profits are taxed on partners' personal returns, avoiding a corporate tax). And with a solid partnership agreement, you can define how you share profits and responsibilities. But **without liability protection, a general partnership is high risk**. Most experienced founders will quickly formalize into an LLC or LLP to get that liability shield.

If you do operate as partners, consider at least a written agreement and plan to upgrade your structure soon. *Two heads are better than one* for brainstorming — but for liability? Two targets with no armor is not a great plan.

Limited Liability Company (LLC) — The Versatile Shield

Now we're talking real protection: the **LLC** is like strapping on a solid shield. It's the go-to armor for many new businesses, and for good reason. An LLC (Limited Liability Company) creates a **separate legal entity** — a wall between your business's actions and your personal assets.

If your LLC faces a lawsuit or debt, your personal belongings are typically safe (so long as you run the business properly and don't mix personal and company funds). This liability protection gives immense peace of mind, like a shield absorbing hits so *you* don't have to.

LLCs are also super **flexible**. Tax-wise, by default a single-member LLC is taxed like a sole prop, and a multi-member LLC like a partnership (pass-through) — *but* an LLC can also choose to be taxed as an S-Corp or C-Corp if that suits better. It's like a game character that can change class — very adaptive.

Fewer formalities are required than a corporation: you typically don't need a board of directors, shareholder meetings, or heavy paperwork to maintain an LLC. This makes it **ideal for small to medium businesses** that want protection *without* a ton of admin burden.

Evelyn, for instance, could form **Evelyn's Fitness LLC** and instantly give her business a more professional image and legal safety. Clients see a company name (boosting credibility), and she sees peace of mind. The LLC is truly the **entrepreneur's trusty armor** — rugged yet nimble. No wonder it's wildly popular as a first formal structure.

C Corporation — The Armored Tank

Next up is the heavy-duty gear: the **C Corporation**. This is the equivalent of an **armored vehicle** on the business battlefield — powerful and robust, but with some weight and cost.

A C-Corp is a completely independent legal entity separate from its owners (shareholders). That means strong **liability protection** — generally, *shareholders can't be held personally liable* for the debts or lawsuits of the corporation. The corporation itself can own property, enter contracts, sue and be sued.

It's like a tank that continues rolling regardless of who's driving — **ownership can change (shareholders come and go) and the corporation lives on**. This structure is favored by larger businesses and startups with big growth plans. Why? Because **investors love C-Corps**. They can issue stock to potentially unlimited shareholders, making it easier to raise capital.

Many venture capital firms and angel investors *insist* on a Delaware C-Corp before they invest — it's the standard for high-growth startups, offering familiarity and a well-developed legal framework. A C-Corp also has the most credibility; having "Inc." or "Corp." in your name can lend weight when dealing with partners.

Now, the downsides: C-Corps face **double taxation** — the company pays corporate tax on its profits, and then if those profits are distributed to owners as dividends, the owners pay tax again on that income. (In the U.S. as of 2025, the federal corporate tax rate is 21%, plus any state tax, before personal taxes.)

However, early-stage startups often reinvest profits (or don't have much profit initially), so the double-tax bite isn't felt right away. And there are strategies to minimize it (like paying salaries or bonuses).

The other downside is **complexity and formality**: C-Corps require a bit of corporate ceremony — think boards of directors, bylaws, annual meetings with minutes, and more compliance paperwork. It's like maintaining a high-performance vehicle — more upkeep, but it can achieve great speeds.

Use case: If you aim to raise serious investment, issue shares to many people, or even go public someday, the C-Corp is the racecar (or rather, tank) built for that track. As Evelyn's mentor put it, *"If you aim* *to race in Formula 1, you should probably build a Formula 1 car from day one, not a go-kart hoping to upgrade later."*

For Evelyn's fitness app, if she decides to seek venture capital and scale nationally, a C-Corp might be her endgame structure. In the meantime, she could start as an LLC and convert, but starting as a C-Corp from the get-go can save hassle if big growth is the plan.

S Corporation — The Tax-Savvy Variant

The **S-Corporation** isn't a different armor shape, but a special coating on the armor. In fact, an S-Corp is *not* a distinct legal entity type at the state level — it's a **tax status** that either a corporation *or* an LLC can elect with the IRS. By filing IRS Form 2553, a qualifying company opts to be treated as an S-Corp for tax purposes.

So why do this? The S-Corp election is all about **avoiding the double taxation** that plagues C-Corps. An S-Corp passes its income or losses directly to owners' personal tax returns (like an LLC or partnership would), so the business itself typically pays no federal income tax.

In exchange for this tax break, **strict rules apply**: you can have at most 100 shareholders, all of whom must be U.S. citizens or residents; you can only issue one class of stock (no fancy preferred shares for investors); and other companies generally can't own shares. In short, S-Corps are meant for **small, domestic businesses**.

The big benefit for profitable small businesses is potential **self-employment tax savings**. In an LLC or sole prop, all your net earnings are subject to self-employment tax (Medicare, Social Security). In an S-Corp, you are required to pay yourself a "reasonable salary" (which *is* subject to payroll taxes), but any additional profit can be taken as a distribution which is not hit by self-employment tax. This can mean paying less in taxes overall — a nice perk if your business is making steady money.

For example, suppose Evelyn's fitness LLC is netting $200k in profit a year. If she stays an LLC (default taxation), she pays self-employment tax on the whole amount. If she elects S-Corp, maybe she pays herself a salary of $100k (with payroll taxes) and takes $100k as distribution — she'd save on taxes for that $100k distribution (avoiding ~15.3% self-employment tax on it). Over years, that's significant.

However, with great tax power comes responsibility: S-Corps require doing payroll, filing additional forms, and maintaining corporate formalities just like a C-Corp. Plus, remember those restrictions — they don't work if you plan to take on foreign investors or multiple classes of investors (in fact, **no non-US owners allowed** in an S-Corp).

In Evelyn's case, if she keeps the business in the family or with one partner and the profits are high, S-Corp could be a smart option. Many entrepreneurs start as an LLC and later **elect S-Corp status** when it financially makes sense — it's a best-of-both-worlds approach. Think of an S-Corp as a standard corporation with a special diet: lighter on taxes, but you have to keep it within certain lanes (follow all the qualification rules).

Trusts — The Hidden Guardian

Trusts are a unique type of armor — more like a shield **behind** the scenes. You might not think of a trust as a business structure, and indeed, you don't usually start a business with one. But it's important to know they exist, especially for **asset protection and legacy planning**.

A **trust** is a legal arrangement where one party (the *trustee*) holds and manages assets for the benefit of another (the *beneficiary*). You've probably heard of trusts in the context of estate planning (like a parent setting up a trust for a child).

For businesses, **business trusts** or *Massachusetts Trusts* can actually own and operate companies via trustees. Why do that? Potentially to avoid probate (if an owner dies, the trust continues to own the business without needing court processes) and for privacy or specific tax reasons.

More commonly, **asset protection trusts** come into play for entrepreneurs once they've accumulated some wealth. These are special trusts (often set up in certain states like Nevada or South Dakota, or even offshore in places like the Cook Islands) that make it very difficult for future creditors to reach the assets in the trust.

For example, an entrepreneur might put their home or investment portfolio into such a trust; if their business later faces a huge lawsuit, those personal assets are far harder to seize. In essence, trusts add a layer of separation between you and the assets, like a secret vault guarded by a trustee.

It's **advanced armor** — something to consider as your enterprise grows and you think about long-term protection and succession. Most new founders won't use a trust to run the operating business (exceptions exist, like certain real estate ventures using land trusts or business trusts). But as you become successful, *adding* a trust to hold ownership of your company or to shield personal assets can be a wise strategy.

Trusts can be complex and require legal guidance, but they are a powerful guardian in the background. *(We'll dive deeper into trusts for asset protection in a later chapter, but for now, know this piece of the armory exists.)*

Beyond U.S. Borders: A Founder's International Outlook

Evelyn's journey is primarily in the U.S., but what if our founder looks overseas or has international partners? The idea of "business armor" spans the globe — most countries have their own versions of LLCs and corporations. Let's step into a founder's shoes who's thinking internationally and see how some common structures abroad compare:

United Kingdom (UK) — Private Limited Company (Ltd)

The UK's popular entity is the **Ltd** — akin to a blend of an LLC and corporation. It offers limited liability to shareholders (so owners' personal assets are protected, like a corporation) and is taxed at the corporate level (the company pays UK corporation tax on profits, then owners pay tax on dividends).

You can form a UK Ltd online in a matter of days through Companies House for a small fee. It's a tried-and-true structure for everything from local shops to startups. For bigger ventures, the UK also has Public Limited Companies (plc) which are more like U.S. publicly traded companies.

A UK Ltd gives Evelyn (or any founder) a credible, recognized status if she wanted to expand her business to London — it signals, *this is a real company*, which can boost credibility with UK customers and banks. Much like an LLC/C-Corp combo, it provides both liability shielding and an established framework for investment (investors can buy shares of a Ltd).

Germany — Gesellschaft mit beschränkter Haftung (GmbH)

Don't let the long name scare you — **GmbH** translates to "company with limited liability." It's Germany's staple for small and medium businesses, essentially equivalent to an LLC or private company.

A GmbH gives owners (shareholders) limited liability and has a formal share capital (Germany requires a typical GmbH to have €25,000 in stated capital, though not all must be paid upfront). German startups often begin as a GmbH to show seriousness — it's a structure that signals stability.

For larger enterprises or ones that want to trade shares publicly, Germany uses **AG (Aktiengesellschaft)**, similar to a U.S. corporation. If Evelyn launched in Berlin, forming "Evelyn Fitness GmbH" would likely be her path, giving her liability protection and German credibility.

Keep in mind, bureaucracy can be heavier — you'll register with German authorities and follow their accounting rules. But the protection and respect a GmbH commands in Germany are like having certified armor made to German engineering standards.

Asia Examples — Private Limited (Pte Ltd) in Singapore/India

Many countries in Asia follow the "Ltd" model inherited from British influence or have their own twists. In **Singapore**, a *Private Limited (Pte Ltd)* is the most common form for startups — it's essentially a corporation with limited liability, known for a quick and business-friendly setup (Singapore consistently ranks high for ease of doing business).

In **India**, the term *Private Limited Company* also denotes a company with limited liability, but with restrictions on share transfers (not publicly traded) — ideal for startups and family businesses.

Both in Singapore and India, having "Pte Ltd" or "Ltd" after your company's name means you've got that corporate shield and separate identity. Tax regimes differ (Singapore, for instance, has attractive tax rates and incentives for new companies), but the concept is the same: owners aren't personally on the hook for company debts.

If Evelyn expanded her app to Singapore, she might create *Evelyn Fitness Asia Pte Ltd* to tap into local investor funds and talent, all while enjoying Singapore's strong legal system.

Everywhere Else — Similar Armor, Different Labels

Virtually every country has an answer to the LLC/corporation. France has the **SARL** (similar to an LLC), Italy the **SRL**, Spain the **SL**, and so on. The European Union even offers a **Societas Europaea (SE)**, a type of European Company that can operate in multiple EU countries under one unified structure.

In Japan, you'll find the **Godo Kaisha (GK)** which is akin to an LLC, and **Kabushiki Kaisha (KK)**, which is more like a corporation. China has LLCs (□□□□□□) for most businesses, too.

The big picture: the language and requirements can vary, but the core principles — liability protection, taxation, formalities — echo the U.S. structures. One notable difference: the U.S. S-Corp is a bit of an American quirk; other countries don't usually have an exact equivalent pass-through corporation election (though many have special small business tax regimes).

In summary, if you're a founder with global ambitions, understand that your **armor might have a different name abroad, but it serves the same purpose**. Choosing where to incorporate can be a strategic decision involving local taxes, investor expectations, and legal systems.

Some founders of international startups even form a U.S. Delaware C-Corp to attract American investors, then register subsidiaries in each country where they operate. Others do the reverse, forming in their home country and creating a U.S. entity for the American market.

There's no one-size-fits-all for international structure — but knowing the local lingo (Ltd, GmbH, Pvt Ltd, etc.) ensures you won't go into battle unprotected on foreign soil.

Comparison Chart: Finding the Right Fit

Every armor type has its pros and cons. Here's a quick comparison of key factors for each major structure:

Business Structure Comparison Chart

Structure	Liability Protection	Taxation	Pros	Cons	Best For
Sole Proprietorship	None	Pass-through (business income = personal income)	Simple setup, full control, no formal filings	No liability protection, difficult to raise capital	Solo entrepreneurs testing ideas, hobbies
General Partnership	None (joint and several liability)	Pass-through (profits/losses split on returns)	Easy start, combined resources, pass-through taxes	No liability shield, disputes risk, dissolution issues	Small businesses with trusted co-founders temporarily
Limited Liability Company (LLC)	Limited liability	Flexible: pass-through or elect S-Corp/C-Corp	Strong protection, flexible management, credible	Costs, filings, self-employment tax without S-Corp	Small-to-mid-sized businesses and startups
C-Corporation (C-Corp)	Limited liability	Double taxation (corporate and dividends)	Strongest protection, unlimited potential, stock issuance	Admin overhead, double taxation, regulatory scrutiny	High-growth startups aiming for investment or IPO
S-Corporation (S-Corp)	Limited liability	Pass-through (no entity tax, owners taxed)	No double taxation, saves on self-employment taxes	Strict eligibility, less flexible ownership structure	Profitable small businesses saving on taxes
Trusts (Business & Asset Protection)	Liability separation (via trust)	Varies (trust taxable or pass-through)	Asset protection, privacy, estate planning advantages	Complex setup, not suitable for active operations	Asset protection and estate planning for entrepreneurs

(Note: LLPs, LPs, and other variations exist too. For example, professionals (like doctors, lawyers) often use LLPs or PLLCs to limit liability for each other's actions. Nonprofits use 501(c)(3) corporations. And some states offer Series LLCs – one LLC with internal "cells" for liability separation. But the structures above are the major ones most entrepreneurs consider.)

Looking at this chart, you can see the trade-offs clearly. It often comes down to balancing **ease vs. protection vs. growth potential**:

- If you value **ease and are just starting with something small** (and you're not at much risk), a Sole Prop might do – but be ready to upgrade when things get serious.

- If you have **co-founders**, don't stay exposed in a General

Partnership longer than necessary – an LLC can give you both protection and a framework for working together (via an Operating Agreement).

- For most new ventures with any ambition, an **LLC is usually a terrific default**. It gives you liability protection and doesn't lock you out of future options (you can morph it into an S-Corp for tax or even convert to a C-Corp if investors demand it).

- If your **vision is to raise capital, issue stock, or go big**, you might lean toward starting with a **C-Corp** from the beginning. Yes, it's more upfront effort, but many startups consider it the cost of playing in the big leagues.

- For a **profitable, stable small business** (say a consulting firm or a family business generating solid income), an **S-Corp election** can be a sweet spot – you get the liability protection (via being a corporation or LLC) and also save on taxes. Just make sure you follow the rules.

- And as you **accumulate wealth or multiple ventures**, consider trusts or multiple entities. An old adage goes, *"Don't put all your eggs in one basket."* Legally, that can mean don't put all assets in one entity. Savvy entrepreneurs may have an LLC for their business operations, and separate LLCs or trusts for real estate or other assets – so a lawsuit in one doesn't jeopardize everything.

Legal Structure Decision Checklist

How do you decide *your* ideal armor? Here's a handy checklist of questions to guide your decision. As you read through, think about

Evelyn weighing her options – and use the same lens for your own venture:

1. **How much liability risk comes with your business?** High-risk activities (e.g. physical products that could injure, locations where accidents could happen, significant contracts) scream for an LLC or corporation *now*, not later. Lower-risk (e.g. a small online service, no/low liability) might start as sole prop but still plan to upgrade as you grow.

2. **Are you starting alone or with others?** If it's just you, you have flexibility – LLC is a strong choice for solo founders. If you have co-founders, *do not* operate as a simple partnership without protection. An LLC or a corporation will protect each of you from the other's mistakes and provide a clear ownership split. Draft an Operating Agreement (for LLC) or Bylaws/Shareholder Agreement (for corporation) early to avoid misunderstandings.

3. **Do you plan to seek outside investment or bring on additional owners?** If you want to raise venture capital or attract angel investors, a Delaware C-Corp is often the required route. Investors like the structure of C-Corps (especially for issuing stock and stock options). If it's just friends/family money, an LLC can still work (they can own membership interests). But know your growth strategy: *Fundraising = likely C-Corp.* Small team, no big fundraising = LLC could suffice. Also, more than 100 owners or any non-US owners will **exclude S-Corp** as an option (because of IRS rules).

4. **What's your profit outlook and tax strategy?** If you expect to *lose money* the first couple years (common for star-

tups), taxes might not drive your decision (you have no profit to tax). But if you expect to be profitable quickly or you're starting a high-income consulting business, think tax strategy. An **S-Corp election** (whether you start as an S-Corp or as an LLC and elect S status) can save on taxes once your net profits are beyond what a "reasonable salary" for you would be. If profits will be modest or you want to reinvest everything, an LLC (default tax) or C-Corp (to potentially retain earnings at a flat corporate tax rate) could work. Consult an accountant if unsure – a little tax planning goes a long way.

5. **How important is simplicity vs. formality for you?**Be honest with yourself: will you keep up with annual meeting minutes, separate financials, and paperwork? If the thought makes your eyes roll, lean LLC. It's more forgiving on formalities (though you *still* must separate finances and follow basic rules). If you don't mind corporate governance and you have a good reason (like investors or certain tax benefits), then a corporation's requirements are fine. Some founders actually appreciate that the formal structure forces discipline – for instance, having to do payroll in an S-Corp can make you more organized.

6. **Where are you doing business? One state or many? U.S. or international?**If you operate only in your home state, forming there is usually best. If you plan to operate or have offices in multiple states, you might form in the most convenient one and register as foreign entity in others. Many startups choose Delaware for its business-friendly laws (especially C-Corps) and then register in their home state too. Internationally, decide if you need a local entity in each country or

if a parent U.S. company owning foreign subsidiaries works. Also, check if your desired structure is available to you: e.g. U.S. S-Corp status has citizenship restrictions; some countries require a local director or have capital requirements (like Germany's €25k for GmbH). These practical factors can influence your choice.

7. **Is this business your *everything* or more of a trial run?**If it's your big passion project that you aim to grow long-term, invest in a solid structure now (LLC or Corp). If it's an experiment or side hustle, you might start as a sole prop for a short while, but set clear milestones (e.g. "if I earn $X or sign Y clients, I form an LLC"). Don't let a temporary status become permanent out of inertia – remember the risks. As one mentor advised, *"Don't wait for a storm to build an umbrella."* Protect yourself before you desperately need to.

8. **Do you have significant personal assets or other businesses to protect?**If yes, lean strongly towards an LLC or corporation from day one. Also consider using multiple entities: for example, if you have a rental property business and a separate consulting business, **keep them in separate LLCs** so a lawsuit in one doesn't threaten the other. If you've built personal wealth, maybe even explore trusts or holding companies to further separate and protect assets. High-net-worth entrepreneurs often use a combination of LLCs and trusts to create legal "firewalls" between ventures.

9. **Future flexibility: can the structure change later if needed?**It's worth noting you *can* change structures later – sole props can form LLCs, LLCs can convert to corporations

(sometimes via a process called statutory conversion or a merger), and small corps can switch between C and S status. But changing can be costly or have tax implications, so try to choose wisely upfront. If you're on the fence, default to the structure that gives you protection now *and* options later. An LLC, for instance, can later become a C-Corp relatively smoothly (this often happens when startups that began as LLCs take VC money; they "flip" into a corporation). Starting as a C-Corp is also fine if you're committed to that path – it's a bit more initial effort, but then you're set for investment. Just avoid being caught in a structure that limits you unexpectedly (for example, an S-Corp that suddenly wants foreign investors – you'd have to drop S status or restructure the company).

10. **Gut check: does this structure align with my vision and values?** This is more intangible, but important. Some founders feel more "official" and motivated when they incorporate – it's a psychological boost that *this is real*. It can impress upon you to take the business seriously. Others might feel weighed down by too much formality too soon. Choose a structure that supports how you want to operate. If calling yourself "CEO of XYZ Corp" energizes you to hustle, go for it. If you prefer saying "owner of XYZ LLC" while you build organically, that's great too. Just don't choose out of fear or misinformation – choose out of intention.

By running through this checklist, you'll likely see a frontrunner structure emerge for your business. And remember, **action beats inaction**. As Jim Rohn wisely noted, *"Whatever good things we build end up building us."* In taking the step to build your business's legal framework, you are also building yourself up as a serious entrepreneur. It's one of those early defining moves that separates the dreamers from the doers.

Embrace the Armor, Build Fearlessly

Evelyn's story comes full circle here. After careful thought, she chose an LLC for her startup – giving her both a safety net and room to grow. She felt a surge of confidence filing the paperwork, like strapping on boots before a long hike. It was no longer "just an idea"; it was a company, *her* company, with a proper foundation beneath it. In the months that followed, that foundation let her take bolder steps – she signed deals knowing her personal savings were safe, she brought on a co-founder under clear terms, and even talked to an investor without scrambling to reorganize the business. Every good structure choice reinforced her credibility and resolve.

As you stand at your own legal crossroads, think of it not as a daunting legal hassle, but as **pouring the concrete for your business's future home**. Yes, it takes a bit of effort now, but it will support everything you build moving forward. The paperwork is finite – the protection and advantages you gain can be lasting. Put on that bike helmet or raise that shield or drive that tank – whatever armor your journey requires – and move forward with confidence. *Setting up the right structure early is an act of entrepreneurship in itself*, a commitment that says: **I'm building something meant to last**. And with that solid start, you can direct your energy to what you do best: growing your business, chasing your vision, and watching your entrepreneurial story unfold, strong and fearless.

6

— • —

THE INCORPORATION DECISION —
DELAWARE, NEVADA, OR WYOMING?

The Founder's Early Crossroads

I closed the book on **Chapter 5** with a critical decision: Treydora would not remain just an idea or a sole proprietorship—it would become a formal company. This moment reminded me of an ancient sailing tradition. Before setting course for undiscovered territories, captains would carefully select their vessel—not just any ship would do for the journey ahead. Similarly, choosing where to incorporate isn't merely a paperwork decision; it's selecting the vessel that will carry your entrepreneurial dreams through calm and stormy seas alike.

I sat at my desk late one night, a cup of coffee growing cold beside me, and realized this *"where"* question carried more weight than I'd expected. Delaware, Nevada, Wyoming—three states kept popping up in every discussion about business incorporation. Each promised something valuable. I felt both excited (Treydora was about to become *official!*) and anxious (one wrong move could mean extra costs or headaches later). In my mind, I sketched out the key factors I needed to consider:

- **Asset Protection:** Would incorporation in a particular state shield my personal assets better if things went wrong? I wanted the strongest protection possible—Treydora was my dream, but I couldn't risk my life savings beyond what I invested.

- **Investor Expectations:** I knew that if I ever sought venture capital or big investors, they might have a preference. Many seasoned investors practically **expect** startups to be Delaware corporations. Would choosing another state raise eyebrows or complicate funding?

- **Privacy:** How public did I want my information? Some states offer more anonymity for owners. As a first-time founder, the idea of keeping a low profile had its appeal.

- **Costs:** Money was tight. Filing fees, taxes, and ongoing compliance costs vary by state. A difference of a few hundred dollars could mean another month of runway for Treydora. I needed a place that fit my budget now *and* in the long run.

- **Long-Term Vision:** Where did I see Treydora in 5 or 10 years? If everything went right, would our state of incorporation still serve us well? I had to align this decision with the big picture—going national or even global one day.

Location Logic: "Where you plant your business flag isn't just about taxes or fees—it's about setting the stage for your company's entire legal and financial future. Choose deliberately, not merely conveniently."

Armed with these criteria, I set out to weigh **Delaware, Nevada, and Wyoming** as the potential home for Treydora. What followed was a blend of research, soul-searching, and a bit of mentorship from those who had walked this path before me.

"Decisions define destinies." I remember jotting these words in my journal. *Choosing where to incorporate felt like choosing the soil in which to plant a young tree. I wanted Treydora to have the best chance to take root and flourish.*

The Three Dimensions of Incorporation

As I weighed my options, I realized that incorporation decisions operate across three crucial dimensions that every founder must consider:

1. The Protection Dimension: How effectively will this legal structure and jurisdiction shield what you've built? This includes asset protection, liability limitations, and the strength of the "corporate veil" in various scenarios.

2. The Growth Dimension: How well will this structure support your specific growth trajectory? Will it facilitate investment, expansion, acquisition, or whatever path you envision?

3. The Identity Dimension: Often overlooked but equally important—how does this choice reflect and reinforce who you are as a founder and what your company stands for?

When these three dimensions align, you've found your ideal incorporation home. When they conflict, you must prioritize based on your unique circumstances and vision.

Delaware: The Gold Standard for Startups

"If you want big investors, go Delaware," my mentor told me over the phone. Delaware is often called the **corporate haven**—more than half of U.S. publicly traded companies and Fortune 500 firms are incorporated there. I recalled reading that fact and thinking: *All those successful companies—they must know something.* Indeed, Delaware's reputation loomed large: a state with business-friendly laws, a well-oiled legal system for companies, and the prestige of being the default choice for ambitious startups.

The Psychology of Incorporation: Beyond the Rational Factors

There's an aspect of the incorporation decision rarely discussed in business books: the psychological impact your choice of jurisdiction can have on you as a founder.

I've observed a fascinating pattern when mentoring entrepreneurs through this decision. Founders often select jurisdictions that subconsciously reflect their business identity and values—and this alignment can actually influence their follow-through and commitment.

For example, founders who choose Delaware often identify with establishment credibility and professionalism. They tend to be more diligent about corporate formalities and governance, perhaps because Delaware's business-serious reputation subtly influences their behavior. These founders typically invest more in professional advisors and take board meetings more seriously from day one.

Conversely, founders who choose Wyoming or Nevada often identify with independence, privacy, and efficiency. They tend to run leaner operations, focus more on bootstrapped growth, and sometimes display greater risk tolerance in their business decisions—mirroring the frontier spirit these states represent.

This isn't merely correlation—our choice of jurisdiction actually shapes our founder identity in subtle ways. I've seen entrepreneurs standing taller and speaking more confidently about their venture after receiving that Delaware certificate, almost as if being part of that business ecosystem granted them new credibility.

Consider not just the technical aspects of your incorporation choice, but how that choice aligns with and reinforces the type of founder you aspire to be.

Why Delaware Tempted Me (Pros & Cons)

On paper, Delaware had a lot going for it:

- **Pro-business Legal System:** Delaware's Court of Chancery specializes in business cases and uses judges who are experts in corporate law (no juries). That means if Treydora ever faced a lawsuit or investor dispute, we'd be in a court that *"speaks business"*. The predictability of outcomes is high because Delaware has decades of legal precedents. For a founder, that translates to peace of mind—fewer legal gray areas.

- **Flexible Corporate Laws:** Delaware would let me form a one-person corporation if I wanted—I could be the shareholder, the director, and the officer all at once. That's perfect for a small startup like Treydora. The laws also allow bylaws and provisions that limit directors' liability, meaning as a founder I'd be somewhat shielded from certain lawsuits as long as I acted in good faith.

- **Tax Advantages (with a Catch):** Here's a neat perk—if your Delaware corporation doesn't actually do business **in Delaware**, the state won't charge corporate income tax. Treydora's operations were going to be elsewhere (my home state), so in theory, we'd pay $0 in Delaware corporate taxes. Delaware also has **no sales tax** and no tax on intangible assets like patents or trademarks, which felt tailor-made for a tech startup. The catch? Delaware does have an **annual franchise tax** for the privilege of being incorporated there. It's at least $175 a year for corporations (and a flat $300 for LLCs), and it can be higher if you authorize millions of shares (common for startups planning multiple investment rounds). I had to consider that ongoing cost, though many founders see it as a small price for Delaware's benefits.

- **Investor Magnet:** Perhaps the biggest draw was investor perception. As I suspected, venture capitalists *love* Delaware C-corps. It's the entity type and location they know and trust. In fact, many VC firms outright require a Delaware C-corporation before they invest. I imagined a future pitch to investors: I didn't want "we're an LLC from Wyoming" (however great that can be) to raise questions. **Treydora, Inc. (Delaware)** just sounds right for the big leagues. This pro weighed heavily in Delaware's favor.

But Delaware wasn't all upside. I also noted a few potential downsides from my perspective:

- **Costs for Small Fish:** For a tiny startup, Delaware's fees can feel steep. Beyond the franchise tax, incorporating there meant I'd likely have to hire a **registered agent** in Delaware (since I didn't live there) and pay that agent every year. Also, because Treydora would actually operate in my home state (not Delaware), I would need to **foreign-qualify** in my state—essentially registering Treydora to do business there and paying my state's fees too. That's double the filings (and costs) each year. The idea of annual reports and fees in two states made me hesitate.

- **Not Privacy-Focused:** Delaware is business-friendly but not particularly privacy-focused. While I wouldn't have to publicly disclose all shareholders or anything (no state requires that level of transparency on day one), Delaware wasn't known for letting you remain as "behind the scenes" as Nevada or Wyoming. This wasn't a deal-breaker, but as a first-time founder I noted it: Delaware prioritizes corporate governance and investor confidence over anonymity.

- **Potential Overkill?:** A part of me wondered, *Do I really need Delaware right now?* If Treydora stayed a small, close-ly-held company for years, some say Delaware's advantages (like the Chancery Court) might never really matter. After all, if you're not suing or being sued and you aren't raising big VC rounds immediately, Delaware could be more firepower (and complexity) than necessary. I had to be honest about my **long-term vision**: I was aiming high, so maybe it wasn't overkill at all—just early preparation.

Emotionally, Delaware felt like the **"safe, conventional"** route for a serious startup. Part of me took comfort in following a well-trod-den path—if thousands of founders chose Delaware, I'd be in good company. Another part of me bristled at the conformity of it; entre-preneurship is about breaking molds, so why was I inclined to just do what everyone else did? I had to remind myself that sometimes the crowd is right, especially when it's the crowd of successful predeces-sors.

I scribbled a note to myself: *"Go where the money flows and the law is tested."* Delaware had both money and legal precedent flowing through it. That thought gave me confidence—it aligned with Trey-dora's big aspirations.

What It Takes: Incorporating in Delaware (Step-by-Step)

To better visualize the Delaware route, I outlined the actual steps I would need to take to incorporate Treydora in Delaware. Writing it down made it real and showed me it was manageable, not some mysterious process. Here's the roadmap I came up with:

1. **Choose a Business Entity Type:** We already decided on this in Chapter 5—Treydora would be a **C-Corporation** (the standard choice for high-growth startups). Delaware supports LLCs and S-Corps too, but I was set on a C-Corp to align with investor expectations and Treydora's growth plan.

2. **Select a Unique Business Name:** I needed to make sure *"Treydora"* wasn't taken by another Delaware company. A quick search on the Delaware Division of Corporations name database would tell me. Delaware requires the name to be distinguishable from existing entities and to include an appropriate ending like **"Inc."** or **"LLC"** as applicable. (Since I'd be a corporation, **Treydora, Inc.** had a nice ring to it.) If my name was free but I wasn't ready to file immediately, Delaware even allows a name reservation for 120 days for a $75 fee—a handy option, though I was ready to move fast.

3. **Appoint a Registered Agent in Delaware:** By law, Delaware corporations must have a registered agent with a physical address in Delaware to receive official mail and legal papers. Since I don't live in Delaware, I'd hire a professional registered agent service. I found that many services charge around $50–$300 per year for Delaware. (Some popular ones include Harvard Business Services, Northwest Registered Agent, Incfile, etc.) This agent's address would be Treydora's official point of contact in Delaware. It's a simple but crucial step—without an agent, Delaware won't approve your filing.

4. **File the Certificate of Incorporation:** This is the core step where Treydora truly becomes a Delaware corporation. For a corporation, Delaware requires a **Certificate of Incorpo-**

ration (LLCs file a similar document called a Certificate of Formation). In this document, I'd include Treydora's name, the registered agent's info, the purpose of the corporation (I could keep it broad, like "to engage in any lawful business," which is common practice), the total number of shares I'm authorizing, and the name of the incorporator (that's me, or my lawyer if I had one file it). I could file this online through Delaware's website or by mail. The state filing fee for a Delaware corporation starts at **$89** (for a modest number of shares); since many startups authorize millions of shares for future issuance, the fee can be higher, but initially I could keep authorized shares lower to manage costs. Delaware's processing time is usually a week or two, but they offer expedited service (for an extra fee) if you need the company formed in 24 hours or even the same day. I decided I wasn't in *that* much of a rush. Filing the certificate was a moment I anticipated with butterflies—it's the moment Treydora would legally come to life.

5. **Draft Bylaws:** Once the state approves the incorporation, the paperwork isn't over. As a corporation, Treydora needs **corporate bylaws**—an internal document outlining how the company will be governed. Bylaws cover things like how directors are elected, what officers the company will have, how meetings are conducted, and so on. Delaware doesn't require me to file the bylaws with the state; they're for our own use. But they are important for keeping everything organized and legal. Since it was just me at the start, my bylaws would be simple—but it's always good to have these in place (and investors will ask for them later). If Treydora were an

LLC, this step would be creating an **Operating Agreement** instead, to outline ownership and management rules. In Chapter 5, I had weighed these structure differences, and now it was time to put the theory into practice.

6. **Obtain an EIN (Employer Identification Number):** An EIN is like a social security number for the business—issued by the IRS so Treydora can pay taxes, hire employees, and open a bank account. This step is the same no matter what state you incorporate in. I'd go to the IRS's website and fill out the online application (it's free). It asks for the corporation's name, responsible party (me), and some other details. The process issues an EIN immediately online. This was one of those "wow, I really have a company" moments—using an EIN instead of my SSN for business matters felt official.

7. **Initial Board Resolutions and Issuing Stock:** With bylaws in hand and EIN ready, I'd then hold an "organizational meeting" (even if it was just me) to adopt the bylaws and appoint myself (and any co-founders or advisors, if applicable) as initial directors/officers formally. I would also authorize the issuance of stock to the founders. In Treydora's case, I might issue myself, say, 1,000,000 shares as founder's stock. All these decisions would be written in initial corporate minutes or resolutions. Delaware doesn't see these, but they are part of the **corporate records** I should keep.

8. **Delaware Franchise Tax & Annual Report:** Finally, I made a note about ongoing compliance. Every Delaware corporation must file an **Annual Report** and pay the franchise tax each year (by March 1st for the prior year). The

minimum tax for a small corporation is $175 (plus a $50 report filing fee), though if Treydora grew and issued lots of shares, that could go up. LLCs in Delaware pay a flat $300 annual tax. This was an important future to-do: missing the franchise tax can incur penalties and even lead to the company being declared void by the state (yikes!). I set a mental reminder that if I chose Delaware, Treydora, Inc. would need this attention every year.

Going through these steps, I realized something: incorporating in Delaware was **straightforward and methodical**. Yes, there were fees and formalities, but nothing insurmountable. The process actually pumped me up—I could almost see the certificate in my hands. Delaware offered a well-defined path, and that gave me confidence. Still, I owed it to myself and Treydora to consider the alternatives with equal care. So I refilled my coffee mug and turned my attention to the next contender: Nevada.

Nevada: The Lure of Tax Freedom and Privacy

If Delaware was the establishment favorite, **Nevada** felt like the bold outlier—the state known for its glitzy cities and, in the business world, for being a **tax haven within America**. I remembered seeing late-night TV ads and countless online promotions: *"Incorporate in Nevada! No state income tax, no franchise tax, total privacy!"* It sounded almost too good to be true. Naturally, I had to separate myth from reality.

I picked up the phone and called a fellow entrepreneur friend who had chosen Nevada for his business a few years back. His experience was enlightening. *"Nevada's great if you care about keeping a low profile and not paying a dime to the state in income taxes,"* he said. *"But watch out for the fees—they get you elsewhere."* I listened carefully and took notes.

Jurisdiction Judgment: "The jurisdiction you choose isn't just a legal designation—it's a statement about your company's identity, values, and ambitions. Delaware speaks of tradition and investor-readiness; Nevada whispers of privacy and independence; Wyoming embodies efficiency and protection. Choose a home that resonates with who you truly are as a founder."

Weighing Nevada's Appeal (Pros & Cons)

Nevada's selling points are indeed attractive, especially to a scrappy founder like me:

- **No State Corporate or Personal Income Tax:** This is Nevada's headline feature. The state simply doesn't tax corporate profits or personal income. If Treydora made money, Nevada wouldn't take a cut. Also, Nevada has **no franchise tax** on corporations or LLCs. That meant no annual fee just for existing (unlike Delaware's franchise tax). The prospect of legally paying $0 to the state government in taxes was alluring. It's one reason many people call Nevada a domestic tax haven. (Of course, I'd still have to pay federal taxes, and if I operated in another state, that state might tax me—important details that tempered this pro.)

- **Strong Privacy Laws:** Nevada prides itself on **protecting the privacy** of business owners. For example, the state does not require the names of shareholders to be filed with the state, and even officers/directors are not part of public record on the initial filings (you *do* file an annual list of officers, but there are services that can help keep your name off public listings if you really want). My friend mentioned Nevada

even didn't share information with the IRS the way many
states do—since Nevada has no income tax, it has no agreement to hand over data to federal tax authorities. I'm not
looking to hide anything illegal (Treydora will play by the
rules), but I admit the idea of keeping my name off mailing
lists and data brokers had some appeal. As a somewhat in-
troverted founder, I appreciated any extra privacy.

- **Liability Protection & Business-Friendly Laws:** Nevada has a reputation for having extremely **strong corporate
veil protection**. In simple terms, that means it's harder in
Nevada for someone to sue me personally for something
my company did—the law really emphasizes the separation
between owner and company. Nevada's statutes make it difficult to pierce the corporate veil *without a showing of deliberate fraud*. For an LLC, Nevada (like Wyoming) only allows **charging orders** as a remedy for creditors—preventing
them from taking over the company even if an owner has
personal debts. Additionally, Nevada's laws are considered
very management-friendly, giving a lot of discretion to directors and officers. This put me at ease that if I made a business judgment that turned out bad, Nevada courts would be
unlikely to second-guess me as long as I acted in good faith.

- **No Residency or Physical Office Required:** I learned I
didn't have to live in Nevada or have an actual office there to
incorporate (same with Delaware and Wyoming, by the way).
I could hire a Nevada registered agent and use a virtual office
if needed. So physically, it was as easy as Delaware to set up
despite me being out of state. This was good to know.

All of that sounded fantastic, but I had to consider the other side of the coin—where might Nevada be less ideal?

- **Higher Initial and Ongoing Fees:** Here was the kicker: while Nevada doesn't take your money via taxes, it does charge hefty **fees** for business filings. My research (and my friend's laments) revealed that incorporating in Nevada comes with an upfront package of fees that significantly exceeds Delaware or Wyoming. For instance, Nevada requires a business to file an **Initial List of Officers/Directors** and a **State Business License** *at the time of incorporation*. These aren't optional—they're mandated filings. The Initial List costs $150 and the Business License is a whopping $500 for corporations. Add the basic filing fee for the Articles of Incorporation (around $75 for a standard filing) and Nevada was looking at roughly **$725 just to start** (for a corporation). For LLCs, the totals were a bit lower (about $425 to start, since the state business license for an LLC is $200 instead of $500). And each year, guess what? You must renew that state business license (another $500 every year for a corporation) and file an Annual List ($150 each year). That's ~$650 per year ongoing. Compared to Delaware's minimum $225/year for a small corp, Nevada could actually cost more annually. This was a big consideration for my budget. Nevada was *"tax free"* but certainly not *"fee free."*

- **Investor Perception and Prestige:** I circled back to the investor question. While no investor would refuse to talk just because of the state of incorporation, I knew Delaware is the gold standard for venture-funded startups. Incorporating in Nevada might raise questions like *"Why?"* or *"What's* *the benefit?"*—questions I'd have to justify in a pitch. Some might even worry I was trying to be too clever with taxes, or that I was a novice who didn't follow the usual path. It might not be a huge problem (especially if I could always re-incorporate or flip into Delaware later), but it gave me pause. The *prestige factor* of Delaware vs. the *privacy/tax factor* of Nevada was a classic trade-off. One article I read even mentioned that having "Inc. in Delaware" carries a certain cachet and reassurance to partners and customers. Was I willing to give that up for some privacy and a state tax break I might not even fully enjoy if I was operating elsewhere?

- **Double Registration if Out of State:** Similar to Delaware, if I incorporated in Nevada but ran the business from my home state, I'd need to register Treydora as a foreign company in my state anyway. So I wouldn't escape my home state's taxes or reporting. Essentially, Nevada's benefits mainly apply if you truly operate in Nevada *or* if your home state also has no corporate taxes so you can choose any state freely. In my case, my home state does have taxes and reporting requirements. That meant Nevada's no-tax benefit was somewhat theoretical—I'd still be paying taxes where I earned the income (e.g., if Treydora earned money in other states, those states could tax it). This realization tempered my excitement about "no corporate tax" in Nevada. It's fantastic if you're physically there; if not, you might be paying someone else instead of Nevada.

- **Legal System Less Proven for Startups:** Nevada does have business courts and is considered business-friendly, but it doesn't have the century of corporate case law that Delaware does. Some attorneys feel Nevada's laws haven't been *as* deeply tested in court. Practically, this might never matter for Treydora, but it was something to note: Delaware's predictability vs. Nevada's relative newness in some areas. Nevada's courts *do* try to be efficient (they even provide early case management for business disputes to keep things moving), which is great. It's just that if I ever needed nuanced legal guidance, I'd find more of it in Delaware's extensive history.

Emotionally, considering Nevada put me at a crossroads of philosophy: Was I building Treydora to "stay hidden and save money," or to "shine bright and attract big opportunities"? Nevada represented the former: a lean, private approach, guarding every dollar. There's something very entrepreneurial about that—every dollar saved is a dollar to fight another day. I was enticed by the idea of never paying a state franchise tax or income tax. It felt scrappy and efficient. Plus, Nevada's strong stance on privacy made me feel secure; I valued my personal information and had heard one too many stories of founders getting unsolicited calls or spam once their business info became public.

On the flip side, I had to check myself: Treydora's mission was to *make an impact*, not hide in the shadows. If a slightly more expensive state like Delaware would grease the wheels of growth (with investors, partners, etc.), maybe that investment was worth it. I also thought about company culture and identity—incorporating in Nevada might subtly signal that saving on taxes was a top priority. Incorporating in Delaware might signal that we're aiming to be a major player. It's funny how a legal formality can carry psychological weight, but it does.

A mentor's words echoed in my mind: *"Don't be penny-wise and pound-foolish."* In other words, saving money in the short term is great, but not if it costs you big opportunities in the long run. I had to ensure any decision for Nevada was driven by strategy, not just the allure of saving a few bucks.

What It Takes: Incorporating in Nevada (Step-by-Step)

I decided to map out Nevada's incorporation process just as I did Delaware's. This way, I could directly compare the effort and requirements involved. It turned out that the steps were similar in many ways, with a few Nevada-specific twists:

1. **Choose the Business Structure:** Nevada, like Delaware, allows various entity types. Many small business owners opt for **LLCs** in Nevada because of the strong liability protection and pass-through taxation (and the $200 annual license instead of $500). However, given Treydora's goals, I was considering a **C-Corporation** here as well. (Nevada also supports S-Corps if you meet IRS criteria, but S-Corps have shareholder limits and other restrictions that didn't fit my vision.) This step was essentially already done in Chapter 5—I wanted a corporation, regardless of state.

2. **Choose a Business Name:** Nevada requires a unique business name distinguishable from other Nevada businesses. It also has rules about including a designator like *Inc.*, *Corp.*, *LLC*, etc., in the name, and avoiding certain restricted words (like "Bank" or "University" unless you have permission). I'd use the Nevada Secretary of State's **Business Entity Search** tool to make sure "Treydora, Inc." was available in Nevada. If by some chance it wasn't, I might have to come up with a variation or a different name. (Thankfully, Treydora is pretty unique.) Nevada allows name reservations too, for ~$25 for 90 days, but again I planned to file right away if I chose this route.

3. **Appoint a Registered Agent in Nevada:** Just like Delaware, Nevada law says you must have a registered agent with a physical Nevada address to receive lawsuits and official notices. I don't live in Nevada, so I'd hire a registered agent service there (usually $100 or less per year). Interestingly, some Delaware registered agent companies have branches in Nevada, so I could use the same provider if I wanted. Being your own agent is only possible if you actually reside in Nevada. Since I didn't, I marked this step: find a good Nevada registered agent (my friend recommended one he used in Las Vegas).

4. **File Articles of Incorporation (and Initial Reports):** This is where Nevada's process differs from Delaware's. To form Treydora as a Nevada corporation, I'd file the **Articles of Incorporation** with the Nevada Secretary of State. The Articles include basic info: company name, registered agent, share structure (number of shares, par value), names of directors or incorporators, and so on. Nevada's base filing fee for the Articles is about $75 (it can be higher if you authorize a lot of stock, similar to Delaware's variable fee). But **simultaneously**, Nevada requires two additional filings:

   ○ The **Initial List of Officers and Directors**—basically a form where you list the key people in the corporation (or managers/members for an LLC). This has a $150 filing fee and is due within 30 days of forming the company. Nevada makes it easy by letting you file it together with the Articles online, so I'd just prepare it upfront.

   ○ The **State Business License Application**—every

Nevada business must have a state business license. For a corporation, the license fee is $500 (for an LLC, it's $200) and it's renewed each year. I would file for this license at the same time as the Articles as well.

Nevada has an online portal called **SilverFlume** where you can do all these filings in one go. If I went this route, I'd brace my credit card for a ~$725 charge covering the Articles, Initial List, and License. The processing is pretty fast—often a few business days if done online. Getting this done would be a milestone: Treydora would become *Treydora, Inc. (Nevada)* and I'd get back a stamped Articles of Incorporation and a Nevada Business License certificate. Despite the cost, the efficiency of Nevada's one-stop filing did appeal to my need for speed.

1. **Draft Bylaws or Operating Agreement:** As a corporation, Treydora would need bylaws in Nevada just as it would in Delaware. No difference here—I'd draft the corporate bylaws outlining how Treydora is governed. If Treydora were an LLC, I'd create an Operating Agreement. Nevada doesn't ask to see these, but having them is part of keeping our liability shield strong (especially in Nevada, where observing formalities helps maintain that strong corporate veil).

2. **Obtain an EIN:** The IRS process for the EIN doesn't care that it's Nevada—it's the same nationwide. So I'd obtain Treydora's EIN online, quickly and for free. Easy win. After filing in Nevada, I could do this step the same or next day to get Treydora ready for banking and hiring.

3. **Initial Corporate Formalities:** Similar to Delaware, I'd hold a meeting (or sign a written consent) to officially ap-

point directors and officers, adopt the bylaws, and issue shares. Nevada corporations have to issue stock and often create stock certificates for each shareholder (at least internally). I pictured myself issuing that first stock certificate to myself—in Nevada, with its asset protection ethos, it felt almost symbolic, like the state saying "your ownership is secure."

4. **Register for Nevada State Taxes/Permits:** Now, Nevada might not have income tax, but if Treydora, say, sold products in Nevada, we'd need a sales tax permit. Also, Nevada has a **"Commerce Tax"** for businesses with gross revenue over a certain amount (currently over $4 million)—basically a tax on big businesses. I made a note that if Treydora ever got *that* big (fingers crossed!), we'd have to file a commerce tax return. In the short term, compliance in Nevada mostly meant remembering to renew that **Annual List** and **Business License** each year. The Annual List updates the state on our officers/directors and costs $150; the Business License renewal is $500 each year for a corporation. These would be due on the anniversary of our incorporation. Missing them could result in fines or the business license getting revoked, effectively shutting down our legal right to operate in Nevada. Clearly, if I chose Nevada, I'd need to stay on top of these yearly tasks. (I set a calendar reminder in advance, just in case.)

Spelling out Nevada's process made one thing obvious: **Nevada was a bit more expensive and paperwork-heavy upfront,** but after that, it was mostly just yearly maintenance and otherwise business as usual. I could handle the steps, no doubt. The bigger question remained: *Did Nevada's benefits outweigh its drawbacks for Treydora?*

I took a deep breath, stretched my legs, and looked at the scribbles covering my notebook. Two states down, one to go. It was time to explore the third option—a state that many consider a hidden gem for entrepreneurs: Wyoming.

Wyoming: The Underdog with Mighty Protections

Wyoming might not come up in everyday startup chatter as often as Delaware or Nevada, but in my research it kept appearing as the **"best kept secret"** for small businesses. In fact, Wyoming was the pioneer that introduced the LLC to the United States back in 1977, and it has been innovating in business law quietly ever since. I was intrigued by what I'd heard: ultra-low fees, no taxes, strong asset protection, and even allowance for anonymous companies. Could this unassuming state offer Treydora the optimal launchpad?

I recall an afternoon scrolling through a startup forum, where a founder proudly claimed, *"I formed my company in Wyoming for $100 in 10 minutes, and I pay just $50 a year. It's the best!"* At first, I was skeptical—was Wyoming really that easy and cheap? But the more I dug, the more I found a lot of love for Wyoming among savvy entrepreneurs, especially those who wanted a simple, affordable way to get started and stay protected.

Frontier Framework: "Wyoming's approach to business formation embodies the frontier spirit—minimal interference, maximum independence, and fierce protection of your autonomy. For bootstrapped founders who value self-reliance, this resonates deeply."

Sizing Up Wyoming's Offer (Pros & Cons)

Wyoming's advantages from a founder's perspective came into focus:

- **No State Taxes (Across the Board):** Like Nevada,

Wyoming imposes **no corporate income tax and no personal income tax** on its residents or companies. It also has **no franchise tax**. Essentially, Wyoming isn't going to charge Treydora any annual state tax for the privilege of existing. That was huge. The only recurring state cost is a small annual report fee (more on that shortly). If I incorporated in Wyoming and ran the business elsewhere, I'd still have to handle taxes in those other places, but at least Wyoming wouldn't pile on. For a lean startup, this was music to my ears.

- Lowest Fees and Costs: Wyoming boasted the lowest formation and maintenance fees of the three states. To form a Wyoming company, the state filing fee is just $100 (for either an LLC or a corporation in most cases). And the annual report/license fee is minimal—$60 (or $50 if you have very low assets). Compare that to Delaware's $225+ or Nevada's $650 yearly. Over a few years, the savings with Wyoming could be significant. For a self-funded founder, that matters. It felt like Wyoming rolled out the red carpet for small businesses without asking for much in return.

- Strong Asset Protection Laws: If asset protection was a contest, Wyoming often takes the crown. Particularly for LLCs, Wyoming is renowned for having perhaps the strongest protections in the country. It was the first state with LLCs and has refined its laws to guard owners from personal liability and guard the company from outsiders. In Wyoming, if someone had a judgment against me personally, the most they could usually get against my interest in Treydora LLC (if it were an LLC) is a charging order—basically a lien on distributions, not a takeover of my company. That means creditors can't seize the company's assets or force its sale. Even for corporations, Wyoming's laws and courts have a history of respecting the corporate veil as long as you maintain the business properly. Knowing that Wyoming courts prioritize keeping personal and business assets separate gave me a sense of security. It's like a safety net for worst-case scenarios.

- Privacy and Anonymity: Wyoming allows anonymous ownership of companies. This doesn't mean skipping any legal requirements, but it means when you form a Wyoming LLC or corporation, you don't have to list the owners or shareholders in public filings. Typically, you list an organizer or incorporator and a registered agent. The actual owners can remain behind the scenes. This anonymity is completely legal and is meant to protect owner privacy. For example, if I formed Treydora, LLC in Wyoming, the public records might only show "Jane Doe, Organizer" (who could be an attorney or service) and a registered agent's address. My name might not appear anywhere publicly. For a corporation, I might not need to list the initial directors publicly either, just the incorporator. This level of privacy rivaled Nevada's and in some ways was even stronger. Considering how much I value privacy, Wyoming's approach was very appealing.

- Simplicity and Speed: From what I gathered, Wyoming's Secretary of State website is very modern and user-friendly. People raved about how easy it is to file online and get confirmation almost immediately. There's even anecdotal evidence of Wyoming processing new business filings in a day or two. For someone eager to launch, this no-hassle bureaucracy (or lack thereof) was a blessing. Wyoming doesn't require a bunch of supplementary filings like Nevada does—no initial lists, no state business licenses. Just file your company and you're done (aside from the simple annual report later). This minimalism fit the lean startup ethos perfectly.

With such a glowing list of pros, I had to ask: what are the cons? Why isn't everyone just incorporating in Wyoming then? I identified a few considerations:

- Investor Familiarity: Ah, here we go again with the investor theme. While Wyoming is gaining popularity (especially for LLCs), it's still not as common a choice for high-growth startups seeking venture capital. Many investors simply expect Delaware, as mentioned. Now, it's worth noting that some startups do begin as a Wyoming LLC to save costs and then "flip" into a Delaware C-Corp when they raise serious money. That's a viable strategy (Wyoming even makes it easy to move your company or domesticate elsewhere if needed). But doing that conversion is an extra step that could incur legal fees or complexity at a time when you're busy fundraising. I realized that if I started in Wyoming to be frugal, I should be prepared down the road to potentially re-incorporate in Delaware before a big investment. Alternatively, I could try to convince investors that a Wyoming corporation is just as good—but that might be an uphill battle if their lawyers are Delaware-minded. This gave me pause. I wanted to set Treydora up once in the ideal way if possible.

- Seriousness and Perception: Let's face it, outside of savvy entrepreneur circles, telling someone your company is a Wyoming corporation might get you a puzzled look (whereas

Delaware's fame precedes it). There's a minor aspect of prestige or credibility in saying you're incorporated in Delaware, especially in tech or finance industries. Wyoming is logically just as legitimate, but perception can lag logic. I asked myself: does this matter to me? A little, if I'm honest. I imagined putting "Treydora, Inc. (WY)" on a partnership contract with a New York client—would they think we were weird for being in Wyoming? Maybe not, but it crossed my mind that Delaware is essentially invisible (no one questions it), whereas Wyoming might prompt a question or two.

- Legal Infrastructure: Wyoming's legal system is perfectly capable, but it doesn't have the dedicated business court like Delaware's Chancery. The volume of corporate case law in Wyoming is also much smaller. In practice, Wyoming companies often lean on Wyoming's statutes and general principles, sometimes even referring to Delaware case law if needed for guidance. I didn't see this as a big problem for a small company, but it's something larger companies might care about.

- Foreign Qualification Likely: Just like with Delaware and Nevada, if Treydora's actual operations (office, employees) were in another state, I'd have to register as a foreign company in that state anyway. So incorporating in Wyoming wouldn't let me escape my home state's requirements. It would just add Wyoming's own (which, granted, are minimal). I would still have two states in the mix. Some business owners decide it's simpler to just form in their home state unless there's a compelling reason not to. In my case, since I was considering Delaware and Nevada too, the foreign qualification issue was a wash—any out-of-state choice meant dealing with two states. I accepted that as a necessary complexity for whichever non-local state turned out best.

Emotionally, Wyoming appealed to my inner bootstrapping entrepreneur. It was like the underdog friend who offers help without asking much in return. I felt an affinity for Wyoming's vibe: low-key, protective, efficient. It aligned with my desire to build a strong foundation without wasting resources. If I were planning to keep Treydora small and self-funded indefinitely, Wyoming might have been the obvious winner right away.

However, my dreams for Treydora were big. I envisioned courting major clients and perhaps investors who might not appreciate the nuances of Wyoming's benefits. I weighed the risk of starting there and later having to relocate the company's incorporation. Was I trying to save money in the wrong place? Or was Delaware's investor-friendly aura worth the extra cost from the start?

One thought warmed me to Wyoming regardless: if I had not chosen a C-Corp structure (say I was okay being an LLC for a while), Wyoming would probably be my top pick. It's known as the LLC haven for a reason. But Chapter 5's decision was clear about needing a structure that supports outside investment (which LLCs can, but often awkwardly). So I focused on Wyoming as a corporation option—which is still fine, just less common than LLCs there.

I found myself reflecting: "Big vision on a small budget—is there a way to have both?" Wyoming seemed to raise that question. It reminded me of a quote I came up with: "Entrepreneurship is about resourcefulness: using what you have to create what you envision." Wyoming, in that sense, was a very resourceful choice. It gave you most of what Delaware offered (legal protections, flexibility) and most of what Nevada offered (tax and privacy perks) at a fraction of the cost. It was as if Wyoming tried to combine the best of both worlds for entrepreneurs.

What It Takes: Incorporating in Wyoming (Step-by-Step)

To complete my analysis, I outlined the incorporation process for Wyoming as I had for Delaware and Nevada. As expected, it turned out to be the simplest of all three:

1. Choose the Business Structure: Wyoming supports all the usual suspects—LLC, C-Corp, S-Corp, etc. Many experts will tell you Wyoming is ideal for LLCs because of its top-notch LLC laws. In fact, most one-person businesses forming in Wyoming go the LLC route. However, I was evaluating Wyoming for Treydora's corporation as well, to keep apples-to-apples with Delaware and Nevada. (If I later decided an LLC was sufficient for now, Wyoming would likely be the choice due to this advantage.) So structure was already decided: if I went Wyoming now, it'd likely be a Wyoming C-Corporation to preserve that pathway to investors, or perhaps an LLC that I convert to a corporation later if I wanted to start lean and switch when funding comes. I kept both possibilities in mind.

2. Pick a Business Name: Wyoming requires your company name to be unique within the state. I'd check "Treydora" in the Wyoming Secretary of State's business entity search online. Wyoming also needs a designator like Inc. or LLC in the name and disallows names that mislead (no naming my company "FBI Corporation" or something dubious). If the name was available, I could proceed. If I wasn't ready to file immediately, Wyoming lets you reserve a name for $60 for

up to 120 days—a higher reservation fee than other states, interestingly, but I didn't intend to wait that long.

3. Select a Registered Agent in Wyoming: Like every state, Wyoming needs an in-state registered agent with a physical address. I don't live there, so I'd hire a Wyoming registered agent (some charge as low as $25/year—Wyoming has some of the cheapest agent services around!). I even came across services advertising "$99 Wyoming LLC—includes first year registered agent." That was mind-blowingly affordable. The agent's job is straightforward: be available to receive any official notices for Treydora. With that set, I'd be compliant on this front.

4. File the Articles of Incorporation (or Formation): To officially form Treydora in Wyoming, I'd file Articles of Incorporation for a corporation (or Articles of Organization for an LLC) with the Wyoming Secretary of State. This can be done online through Wyoming's business portal. The information required is basic: company name, registered agent info, the names and addresses of incorporators, number of shares (if a corporation), etc. Wyoming's filing fee is a flat $100 for most filings. (Technically, for-profit corporations pay $100 for the first $50,000 of par value of their shares and a bit more if higher, but practically most small corps just pay $100.) The online filing is quick—I could literally do it in 10 minutes. After submission, Wyoming processes it usually in 1-3 business days, and often you can download your approved certificate immediately when it's done. I imagined how easy it would be to see "Treydora, Inc.—Filed with Wyoming on [Date]" pop up in my email. Minimal

hassle, minimal cost.

5. Draft Bylaws or Operating Agreement: As with the others, after forming a corporation I'd create corporate bylaws to govern Treydora. If Treydora were an LLC in Wyoming, I'd definitely draft an Operating Agreement—especially in Wyoming, since part of what gives an LLC its strength is having that agreement to show you're treating it seriously as a separate entity. Wyoming doesn't require filing these documents; they remain internal. Given Wyoming's emphasis on asset protection, I knew I should diligently maintain these records to maximize the liability shield.

6. Obtain an EIN: Next, I'd apply for the EIN via the IRS site (same process as always). Quick and essential. Nothing special to do for Wyoming in that regard. By this point in the process, Treydora would exist as a legal Wyoming entity, and with an EIN we'd be ready for business banking and permits.

7. Comply with Wyoming's Annual Requirements: Wyoming's beauty is its simplicity here. The state has no annual franchise tax, no annual business license fee. Instead, it asks for a short Annual Report each year, which is essentially a fee based on your business's assets located in Wyoming. If you have $0-$250,000 in assets in Wyoming, you pay a flat minimum of $60. Many online businesses or holding companies fall in that minimum bracket. The annual report is due on the first day of the anniversary month of your formation (e.g., if I formed Treydora on April 10, the annual report is due by each April 1). It can be filed online easily. I made a note: Treydora's ongoing Wyoming cost would likely be

just $60 a year—and that's it! Aside from that, I'd maintain a registered agent each year and keep my contact info updated. Wyoming doesn't require any annual list of members or financials or anything. It felt very low-bureaucracy.

8. Additional Setup: After incorporation, I'd hold an organizational meeting (as with the others) to issue stock and officially elect officers. I'd then open a business bank account. Wyoming doesn't have big national banks headquartered there, but I could easily open the account in my home state for Treydora, Inc. (Wyoming)—banks generally accept out-of-state companies as long as you have your EIN and formation docs. Everything after formation would run the same way as any U.S. company.

By the time I finished writing out Wyoming's steps, I was truly impressed. It was no myth—Wyoming was indeed extremely friendly to entrepreneurs. The state combined an almost Nevada-level of tax advantage with even lower fees than Delaware, and legal protections rivaling the best of the best.

I leaned back and smiled. How fortunate was I to have these options! Here I was, a founder with a big dream and limited funds, and I had not one or two but three excellent states vying to be the home of my startup, each with unique merits. I almost wished I could incorporate Treydora in all three simultaneously—but alas, one must choose.

Choice Clarity: "The state you choose becomes part of your company's DNA—not just legally, but culturally and strategically. It's not just about where you file some papers; it's about aligning your business environment with your deepest aspirations."

The Decision — Planting Treydora's Flag

After all the research, late-night pondering, and heart-to-heart talks with mentors and fellow founders, the choice of state ultimately came into focus. In truth, there was no one-size-fits-all answer—it hinged on Treydora's needs and my vision for its future.

I grabbed a fresh page in my notebook and drew a simple table to summarize my thoughts one last time, almost as a checklist:

Factor Delaware — Nevada — Wyoming — "Lean "Corporate "Privacy & Tax Protection" Haven" Haven"

State Corporate Tax No (if no business No No in DE)

Personal Income Tax No No No

Franchise Tax Yes (annual No No franchise tax forcorps)

Upfront Filing Cost Moderate (High (~$725 Low ($100 flat) ~$89 + agent) corp package)

Annual Fees Moderate (min High (~$650 Low (~$60/year) ~$225 corp/year corp/year))

Legal System Best (Chancery Business court General courts Court, vast case (good, but newer) (adequate) law)

Investor Friendly? Yes (VCs Not typically Not typically prefer it) (may raise (might need to flip (YES) questions) later)

Asset Protection Strong (solid Very strong (hard Very strong (esp. corporate law) to pierce veil) for LLCs)

Privacy/Anonymity Moderate (not High (minimal High (anonymous publicizing disclosure, no ownership allowed) owners) IRS sharing)

Best For Going big (IPO, Privacy seekers, Small businesses, large funding risk mitigation bootstrappers rounds)

(I ticked the criteria most important to me: investor friendliness, strong legal protection, and manageable costs.)

Looking at this comparison, I asked myself: What is Treydora's destiny? If I was aiming to build a high-growth startup that would attract major investment and possibly go public one day, Delaware clearly aligned with that path. It offered the predictability and investor appeal that would smooth the journey. Nevada appealed to the part of me that wanted maximum control and privacy, but its high ongoing fees felt like they'd drain a small company without delivering clear benefits unless I was physically in Nevada. Wyoming tugged at my frugality and sense of efficiency—it was nearly ideal for a closely-held company, but I acknowledged that I might outgrow its benefits if venture capital entered the picture.

In the end, I made a decision that balanced long-term vision with present-day practicality: I chose to incorporate Treydora in Delaware. It was the state that best matched where I wanted Treydora to go. I realized that I wanted to pave the runway for Treydora as far as possible, and Delaware's widespread acceptance in the business world would help me do that. It wasn't the cheapest immediately, but it wasn't prohibitively expensive either—and spending a bit more now could prevent costly re-incorporation maneuvers later on.

Emotionally, this decision just felt right. I remember the moment I knew: I was re-reading my notes, and when I envisioned Treydora being a big success, I pictured it as a Delaware company. That mental image sealed it. It was as if Treydora itself was telling me, "Take me where I can fulfill my potential."

Once decided, I acted. Incorporating Treydora, Inc. in Delaware turned out to be one of the most thrilling experiences of my founder journey so far. I went online to the Delaware Division of Corporations, filled out the forms with all the information I had meticulously prepared, and with a deep breath, clicked "Submit." In that instant, Treydora transcended from an idea in my head to a legal entity recognized on paper. I'll admit, I sat there for a minute, a bit stunned. It was done. I had actually done it!

A week or so later, a package arrived from my registered agent. Inside was a freshly stamped Certificate of Incorporation for Treydora, Inc., emblazoned with the Great Seal of the State of Delaware. I held it like a newborn's birth certificate, which in many ways it was. I even took a picture with it! That certificate represented more than just a filing—it symbolized my commitment to this venture. Treydora now had a home and an identity that I could build an empire upon.

I took that certificate and pinned it on the wall above my desk. It's still there as I write this, a reminder of the day I officially became a founder. Every time I glance at it, I feel a surge of motivation: if I could navigate that complex decision and come out the other side, I can handle whatever challenges entrepreneurship throws at me next.

Finally, I sat down to reflect on what I'd learned through this process. It struck me how empowering it was to educate myself on these topics. Incorporation went from being an intimidating legal maze to a series of actionable steps that I executed with confidence. Each state taught me something: Delaware taught me about aligning decisions with vision, Nevada taught me the value of questioning what truly matters (privacy and saving costs vs. broader goals), and Wyoming taught me that sometimes the best solutions are off the beaten path.

Decision Done: "The greatest barriers to entrepreneurial momentum aren't external obstacles but internal hesitation. Make decisions with purpose, act with confidence, and free yourself to focus on what truly matters—building something extraordinary."

Encouragement for the Entrepreneurial Reader

If you've made it with me to this point, you might be weighing your own options, feeling a bit of the same excitement and anxiety I felt. Here's my advice to you as a fellow entrepreneur and friend: take the leap and formalize your dream. Whether you choose Delaware's well-traveled road, Nevada's protective embrace, Wyoming's cost-effective simplicity, or even just your home state's familiarity, the important thing is to make a choice. Don't let indecision or fear of paperwork stop you from moving forward.

In hindsight, incorporating Treydora when I did was one of the best decisions I made. It gave my startup legitimacy. It made opening bank accounts, signing contracts, and building trust with partners so much easier because I wasn't just "Jane with an idea"—I was "Jane, CEO of Treydora, Inc." That shift in mindset is priceless. It made me take myself and my business more seriously.

Remember, no decision is forever. If circumstances change, you can always adapt (businesses can move states, structures can evolve). What matters now is protecting your venture and giving it the platform it needs to grow. The peace of mind I got from knowing my personal assets were shielded and that Treydora had the right foundation was huge. It allowed me to pour 100% of my energy into building the product and acquiring customers, rather than worrying about the "what ifs" of operating as an informal business.

So, here's my challenge to you: Incorporate **your** dream. Go ahead and pick the state that fits your situation best. Use the step-by-step guides in this chapter as a checklist. Take it one step at a time—you'll be amazed at how achievable it is. And when you get that certificate or official paperwork back, celebrate it! You've earned it. It's not just a piece of paper; it's a milestone marking your transition from someone with an idea to the owner of a real, thriving company.

"Every great company began with a courageous decision." Today, you have the chance to make that decision for your own venture. Trust yourself and go for it. Just as Treydora's journey took a giant leap forward when I chose where and how to incorporate, your business's journey will leap forward when you do the same.

Chapter 6 concludes with Treydora, Inc. proudly incorporated and ready to soar. I'm rooting for you as you take this step for your business. Here's to planting your flag and watching your dream grow—the world is waiting for what you'll build next!

7

---·---

FUNDING AND PITCHING WITH PASSION AND PRECISION

The Angel's Perspective: Seeing Your Vision Through Their Eyes

Have you ever had a million-dollar idea—but not exactly a million dollars to make it happen? Welcome to the founder's dilemma. Every successful entrepreneur eventually faces the question of **funding**: where to find the capital and support to transform vision into reality.

One powerful answer often comes in the form of **angel investors**. Angel investors are like master gardeners who specialize in saplings rather than mature trees. While venture capitalists seek established growth with predictable patterns, angels recognize potential in the smallest shoots—sometimes before the first blossom appears. They provide not just water (capital) but also the right soil conditions (guidance) and protection from harsh elements (connections) that allow fragile ideas to take root and flourish into something magnificent.

Don't let the name mislead you—these "angels" aren't celestial beings descending with bags of cash. They're accomplished individuals—often former entrepreneurs or executives—who invest their personal wealth in early-stage ventures. They're nicknamed "angels" because they appear at a pivotal moment: when your startup is too risky for banks yet too early for venture capitalists. In that vulnerable gap between idea and traction, angels provide the runway for lift-off.

"An investor writes the check with their hand, but makes the decision with their heart. Your passion ignites their interest, but your preparation secures their commitment."

Picture this: You're at a local coffee shop, enthusiastically describing your startup concept—perhaps an innovative eco-friendly product. A stranger at the next table leans over and says, "Tell me more." Twenty minutes of animated conversation later, they hand you their card and suggest discussing a $50,000 investment in your vision. That, my friend, is an angel investor in action.

Angels come in all forms—doctors, lawyers, tech pioneers, or successful retirees—but they share one common trait: a passion for spotting the *next big thing* and the courage to back it early. If your idea truly resonates, an angel might appear in the most unexpected places.

What Angel Investors Really Look For

More than anything, angels invest in **people and potential**. They want to see:

- **A Strong Team:** They invest in founders more than ideas. Demonstrate that you and your team possess grit, expertise, and adaptability. Angels need to trust that *you* can navigate the inevitable storms ahead.

- **A Real Market Need:** Your solution should address a tangible problem. If you can prove there's a genuine pain point—and better yet, show early traction like pilot customers or pre-orders—you'll ignite investor interest.

- **Scalability:** Angels dream big. They're excited by solutions that can grow from local niche to global market. If the opportunity is vast, their potential return multiplies accordingly.

- **A Plausible Exit:** Remember, angel funding isn't charity—they eventually want returns. Whether through acquisition or IPO down the road, show that you've thought about how they might realize their investment.

When these elements align, you become magnetic to angel investors. As one seasoned investor explained to a nervous founder at her first pitch:

"Your pitch deck isn't just slides and numbers—it's the movie trailer for your entrepreneurial journey. Show me the highlights, spark my curiosity, and make me want to see the full story unfold."

In this context, your *entire business* is the feature film—but first, you must captivate them with the preview. (We'll explore pitch decks in detail shortly.)

Finding Your Perfect Match

The next challenge: how do you actually meet these elusive angels? Networking is paramount. Many cities have local angel groups that host pitch events and office hours. Industry-specific angels also exist—someone who built their fortune in healthcare might eagerly back the next medtech breakthrough.

Online platforms like AngelList and Gust allow you to showcase your startup profile where angels actively browse for opportunities. However, remember the golden rule: **warm introductions**. A recommendation from a mutual connection or fellow founder will get an angel's attention far more effectively than any cold email. In fact, spamming an investor's inbox with a generic pitch is about as effective as cold-calling the Pope for startup advice—it simply doesn't work.

Instead, focus on building authentic relationships and securing credible introductions. Above all, remember that angel investing is a two-way street. Yes, you need their capital, but angels often become **mentors** and **partners** in your journey.

As Jim Rohn wisely observed, *"You are the average of the five people you spend the most time with."* The right angel can elevate your game by bringing invaluable networks and knowledge. Choose wisely—their influence will shape your startup in ways far beyond mere dollars.

The Power of Alignment: Rob's "SmartHive" Story

Consider Rob, a founder with an unusual concept—a smart beehive sensor that monitors honey production. Every bank deemed this idea too niche and risky. But then Rob met a retired software executive who happened to be an amateur beekeeper. This angel immediately recognized the potential: "Smart beehives could scale globally. Think of the data alone!" he exclaimed.

That alignment of passions created magic. In exchange for a $60,000 investment, Rob offered this angel a modest equity stake. With both the capital *and* the mentor's guidance, Rob refined his technology, secured partnerships with beekeeping suppliers, and within a year, SmartHive sensors were shipping to four different countries.

That's the transformative power of a well-aligned angel investor—when their expertise and enthusiasm meet your vision, a niche concept can blossom into an international business.

"The match between founder and investor is like finding your perfect dance partner. Technical skill matters, but without rhythm and chemistry, you'll step on each other's toes."

From Rob's experience (and countless others), we learn a fundamental lesson: **passion must meet preparation**. Angel investors may be moved by your excitement and story, but they commit because you've done the homework. As one founder put it, angel investing is where "passion meets preparation"—angels respond to your energy, but invest because of your evidence.

Show them you have *both* the fire **and** the roadmap: the vision and the viable plan to execute it. If you take away just one insight about angels, let it be this: **finding an angel investor is about synchronicity—where their resources and mentorship align with your vision and hustle.** When that synchronicity clicks, you'll have the runway needed to truly take flight.

Crafting Your Story: Building a Compelling Pitch Deck

Once you understand what investors seek, it's time to equip yourself with one of the most crucial tools for fundraising: the **pitch deck**. This brief presentation (typically 10-15 slides) tells your business story in a compelling, concise format. Think of it as **the narrative of your startup, distilled into visuals and bullet points**—your movie trailer, designed to captivate investors and leave them wanting more.

Let's continue with Ava, an entrepreneur with a brilliant platform concept that connects remote freelancers with local nonprofits—a "volunteering marketplace." Despite her passion and working prototype, investors weren't lining up. Her mentor advised creating a **pitch deck**, explaining that this would help cut through the noise and present her idea with clarity and impact.

As Ava's mentor explained: *"The pitch deck helps you cut through the noise by delivering a concise, clear narrative. No rambling tangents, no overwhelming data dumps—just the essentials that spark intrigue and open the door to deeper conversations."* In other words, a great deck shines a spotlight on what matters most about your startup.

The Architecture of an Effective Pitch Deck

While every business is unique, most successful decks cover these key elements in roughly this sequence:

- **Title Slide:** Your company name, logo, and a memorable one-liner tagline.

- **Problem Statement:** What pain point or opportunity are you addressing? Clearly articulate the market gap. *Example:* "Nonprofits struggle to find skilled volunteers—an untapped reservoir of talent exists, but there's no efficient way to connect."

- **Solution:** How does your offering solve that problem? Introduce your product or service and its value proposition. *Show* how it addresses the pain point better than alternatives.

- **Market Opportunity:** Who is your target market and how large is it? Investors want to see substantial or growing opportunity. Include your **TAM** (Total Addressable Market) if possible—e.g., "This represents a $5 billion market with 12% annual growth."

- **Business Model:** Explain how you'll generate revenue. Are you charging a subscription, taking a commission, selling a product? Show that you've thought through sustainable income streams.

- **Competition:** Acknowledge the competitive landscape. Who else is tackling this challenge, and how are you different (better, faster, cheaper, or niche-focused)? Highlight your unique advantage or "secret sauce."

- **Traction:** This is where you impress with progress to date—user growth, early customers, partnerships, or product milestones. Even a pilot program or a few enthusiastic early adopters can validate your concept. If you have sales or user metrics, showcase them!

- **Team:** Introduce the key team members and why *you* are the right people to execute this vision. Investors bet on people; highlight relevant experience, expertise, and track record of execution. If you have notable advisors or mentors, include them as part of your team strength.

- **Financials & Forecast:** Provide a high-level view of your financial projections—revenues, expenses, and growth trajectory for the next 3-5 years. Keep it realistic yet ambitious. Also state how much funding you've raised (if any) and how much you're seeking now. Avoid overly optimistic numbers; credibility is key.

- **The Ask (Use of Funds):** Conclude by stating exactly what you're requesting: "We are raising **$X** for **Y%** equity (or as a convertible note), and we will use it to accomplish Z (e.g., scale our platform, hire key team members, expand marketing)." Be specific about how the funds will fuel your next milestones. This clarity demonstrates you have a plan for the capital.

Notice how this structure presents a coherent story: *There's a problem, we have a solution, there's a big opportunity, we know how to execute, and here's proof we're on track—now imagine what we could achieve with your investment.* A well-structured pitch deck is concise, visually engaging, and **narrative-driven.**

"Your pitch isn't a performance—it's a conversation with the future. The best founders don't merely describe what is; they

invite investors to see what could be. They paint reality with such vivid clarity that possibility feels inevitable."

In Ava's case, she kept her deck to 12 clean slides with strong visuals and minimal text. On her "Problem" slide, she painted a picture of a nonprofit manager struggling to find volunteers. On her "Solution" slide, she showed how her app matches skilled volunteers with causes in need, like a dating app for social good. Each slide flowed into the next like chapters in a compelling story.

The Three Minds of Effective Pitching

Throughout my years of pitching and watching others pitch, I've observed that successful founders mentally navigate three distinct psychological states during the process—what I call the "Three Minds of Effective Pitching":

1. The Architect Mind - Before the pitch, this mindset meticulously constructs your narrative, anticipates questions, and ensures every element serves your strategic purpose. The Architect is analytical, thorough, and leaves nothing to chance.

2. The Storyteller Mind - During the pitch, this mindset creates emotional connection and possibility. The Storyteller makes data feel human, turns features into benefits, and transforms abstract concepts into tangible futures.

3. The Partner Mind - During Q&A and follow-up, this mindset demonstrates collaboration and mutual value creation. The Partner shows investors you're someone they want to work with for years—receptive to input while maintaining clear vision.

Most founders naturally excel in one of these minds while neglecting the others. The true masters of fundraising can seamlessly transition between all three, knowing exactly when each mindset serves them best.

Modern Tools for Deck Creation

In today's world, crafting a great pitch deck doesn't mean starting from scratch alone. Entrepreneurs are increasingly leveraging **AI tools** to build decks with both *passion and precision*. For instance, you can use ChatGPT to brainstorm and refine slide content. Feed it a list of bullet points for your "Solution" slide, and ask it to craft a concise, punchy sentence that captures the essence. You might be surprised at the creative phrasings it suggests!

Similarly, design-focused AI tools can help generate slide layouts, color schemes, or even custom icons and graphics to make your deck visually compelling. If you have data to present (perhaps a chart of user growth), AI analytics tools can assist in analyzing the data and producing attractive visualizations for your deck.

These tools can save time and add polish to your presentation, but remember: **AI is a co-pilot, not the captain.** Always review and edit AI-generated content to ensure it's accurate and truly reflects your voice. The heart of your pitch must still come from *you*—your deep understanding of your business and your authentic passion.

Ava embraced all resources at her disposal. She used AI to help tighten the wording on technically complex slides and employed design tools to create a simple logo and visuals. With her refined deck in hand, she *practiced* her presentation relentlessly—in front of the mirror, to her patient dog, and finally to a small group of friends who peppered her with challenging questions. This preparation meant that by the time she faced actual investors, her narrative was smooth and her confidence was steady.

The result? Ava emailed her pitch deck to a local angel network, and within 48 hours received a reply: "We love your concept—can you come pitch to us next week?" That is the power of a clear, compelling pitch deck—it opens doors and creates opportunities. A polished deck demonstrates seriousness and professionalism. It *invites* investors to envision the possibilities. In short, **it helps you stand out**.

As Ava discovered, a great deck saved everyone time by conveying the essentials efficiently while sparking meaningful conversations with investors. It told a story that data alone couldn't express.

Why Investing in Your Pitch Deck Pays Dividends

To recap why putting effort into your pitch deck is worthwhile:

- **First Impressions Matter:** Angels and VCs review count-less pitches. A well-crafted deck immediately shows you're prepared and professional—it sets you apart from those who improvise.

- **Clarity = Confidence:** Organizing your thoughts into a deck forces you to clarify your business model and strategy. That clarity will shine through in your presentation and give investors confidence in your vision.

- **Storytelling Framework:** The deck provides a narrative blueprint. It ensures you cover all critical points while taking the audience on a logical journey from problem to solution to opportunity. It helps make your presentation memorable and coherent.

- **Guide for Discussion:** Even after your presentation, in-vestors will revisit the deck. A great deck continues selling your idea even after you've left the room, as they review your slides and discuss with partners.

- **Confidence Booster:** Finally, *knowing* you have a strong deck behind you can dramatically boost your confidence. It's like having your arguments and visuals perfectly aligned so you can focus on connecting with your audience.

In building your deck, keep Jim Rohn's wisdom in mind: *"Never begin the day until it is finished on paper."* Similarly, never walk into an investor meeting until your plan is clearly laid out—in this case, on the slides of your pitch deck. Complete the preparation on paper (or PowerPoint) first, and you'll be far more precise and persuasive when you pitch.

The Art of Delivery: Presenting With Impact

Having a superb pitch deck is vital, but **how** you deliver that pitch can make the critical difference. Investors don't just invest in concepts; they invest in the person behind them. This is where your communication and storytelling abilities take center stage. The goal is to present with **passion and precision**, leaving the room convinced that you are the one who can transform this idea into a thriving venture.

Think of masterful communicators like Steve Jobs unveiling revolutionary products—the calm confidence, the storytelling arc, the ability to captivate an audience. Jobs treated product launches like theatrical performances, and similarly, pitching your startup is a performance meant to inspire and persuade. As Jobs himself believed, *"The most powerful person in the world is the storyteller."* The person who can tell a compelling story sets the vision and inspires others to follow. In a pitch meeting, **you** are that storyteller. Your words, your slides, and your presence all combine to convey the narrative of your startup and why it matters.

"A pitch is not a monologue about your product—it's a dialogue about possibility. You're not selling features; you're inviting investors into a vision of what could be, with their help."

So, how can you deliver the perfect pitch? Here are key strategies, inspired by expert communicators and presentation coaches:

Open With a Hook

First impressions form in seconds. Don't begin with a dry introduction of yourself or your company. Instead, hook the audience immediately—perhaps with a startling statistic, a thought-provoking question, or a brief anecdote.

For example, if Ava were pitching her nonprofit volunteer platform, she might start with: "Last year, over 5 million skilled professionals wanted to volunteer but couldn't find the right opportunity. Imagine the impact if we could connect even a fraction of them to nonprofits in desperate need." A strong opening commands attention.

In pitching parlance, this is often your **elevator pitch**—a concise, passionate summary of your business that sparks interest in the first minute. Don't hesitate to be emotional in framing the problem; remember Zig Ziglar's insight: *"People don't buy for logical reasons. They buy for emotional reasons."* Investors are people, and a story that resonates with their emotions or imagination will stick. Hook them early, so they *must* hear the rest of your story.

Tell a Story, Don't Just Recite Facts

Humans are wired to respond to narratives. Rather than simply listing facts about your product, weave those facts into a compelling story. Introduce a relatable character or scenario. You might share the **founding story**: what inspired you to start this company?

Perhaps: "I was a nonprofit manager myself, frustrated by how hard it was to find volunteers with the exact skills we needed, so I decided to solve that problem..." By personalizing the journey, you create empathy and credibility.

In your narrative, highlight the conflict or challenge (the problem you set out to solve) and then the resolution (your solution). This mirrors the classic story structure of setup → conflict → resolution, which naturally engages listeners. Public speaking expert David JP Phillips emphasizes structure and simplicity as vital elements of a compelling presentation—**clear narratives with a beginning, middle, and end, supported by simple, powerful visuals, will keep your audience captivated by your story.**

Make your slides reinforce your narrative rather than distract from it. A brief customer anecdote or use-case scenario can be remarkably effective: "Meet Jane, a talented graphic designer who wanted to volunteer but couldn't find the right opportunity—until she found our platform and connected with a charity that needed her exact skills, helping them raise donations with her powerful designs." Now your pitch isn't just abstract; it's humanized.

Be *Passionately* Authentic

Passion is contagious. Let your enthusiasm for your venture shine through. Speak with conviction and energy. If you truly believe in your solution, convey that emotion. Investors often say they bet on the jockey (the founder), not just the horse (the idea). They want to see that fire in your eyes.

That said, passion must be balanced with **professionalism and clarity**. Maintain steady eye contact, use open body language, and project confidence. Even if you're nervous inside, focus on communicating clearly and warmly. One technique is to channel your nerves into excitement—physiologically, they're remarkably similar feelings.

Remember, **confidence isn't about having no fear; it's about proceeding in spite of it.** As Zig Ziglar noted: *"For every sale you miss because you're too enthusiastic, you will miss a hundred because you're not enthusiastic enough."* In other words, err on the side of showing you care deeply. If you don't exude belief in your own idea, you can't expect investors to believe in it either.

Keep It Concise and Conversational

A common mistake is trying to cram every detail into your pitch. But an investor presentation is not a dissertation defense. It's advisable to **keep your presentation to about 5--10 minutes**, hitting the key points outlined in your deck. Use simple language, not jargon, especially if some investors might not be experts in your domain.

You can always provide more technical details or specific answers during Q&A. During the pitch, aim to convey the essence, not every minor detail. Speak in a conversational tone as if you were explaining your idea to a smart friend, not lecturing in a classroom. This makes you more relatable and your content more digestible.

"A great pitch has the precision of a surgeon and the warmth of a storyteller. Cut straight to what matters, but do it with heart."

Use Your Voice and Body Effectively

Public speaking is a performance art. Pay attention to your **tone, pace, and body language**. Vary your vocal pitch and volume to avoid a monotonous delivery—lower your voice when saying something serious, and brighten it when sharing something exciting. Use pauses strategically: a brief silence after a key point allows it to sink in (and conveys confidence).

Stand with relaxed purpose, and don't be afraid to move naturally or gesture to emphasize points. Your physical presence projects confidence (or lack thereof). Importantly, **smile** when appropriate—it builds connection and shows you're comfortable. If you appear at ease and enthusiastic, your audience will feel engaged and intrigued.

Invite Imagination Through Imagery

Great presenters often ask rhetorical questions or use visual language. For example, "Imagine a world where finding a volunteer is as easy as hailing a ride on Uber—that's what we're building." Such phrases encourage listeners to picture the impact themselves, actively engaging their imagination.

Storytellers advise "show, don't tell." While you're telling, also show: use your slides to display powerful images or, better yet, a brief demo of your app if possible. Seeing a product in action or a before-and-after scenario can be incredibly persuasive.

Throughout the pitch, maintain an underlying thread: **why *you* and *why now*.** Reinforce why you and your team are uniquely positioned to solve this problem—perhaps your background or how you came together driven by a common mission. And why now is the time—maybe the market is ready or technology has evolved making your solution possible. This creates urgency and inevitability: if this change is going to happen sooner or later, the smart money would rather back you *now*.

Finally, **practice, practice, practice**. No one delivers a perfect pitch by accident. Rehearse your presentation multiple times. Practice in front of a mirror to observe your body language. Rehearse before colleagues or friends and welcome their feedback. Have them ask tough questions so you can practice thinking on your feet. The more you practice, the more your confidence will grow, and the more natural your delivery will become.

Preparation is the foundation of precision—it allows you to be fully present and passionate in the moment because you're not struggling for what to say next.

In sum, delivering the perfect pitch is about **connection**—connecting your story to the investor's emotions and logic. It's performing, but it's also *being authentic*. Genuine passion is your greatest asset; speak from the heart, backed by thorough preparation.

As one final tip, end your presentation on a strong note. Don't trail off with "Well, that's about it." Instead, finish with a confident call-to-action or a memorable statement of your vision: "Together, we can help millions of skilled professionals volunteer and transform communities—and that's a future we're inviting you to create with us." Then thank the audience. A confident close leaves a lasting impression.

To quote another master motivator, Zig Ziglar: *"You don't have to be great to start, but you have to start to be great."* When it comes to pitching, this means you might not be a *perfect* presenter yet, but you have to start pitching to become great at it. With each presentation, you'll improve. So embrace the opportunity and step forward with confidence.

The Crucible: Navigating Investor Questions

You've captivated the room with a well-structured pitch delivered with passion—congratulations! Now comes perhaps the most critical part of the process: the **Q&A session**. In many ways, how you handle investors' questions can seal the deal or break it. This is where investors dig deeper, test your knowledge, and observe how you think on your feet. It can feel intense, but it's also an opportunity to showcase your mastery and character.

First, reframe how you view questions: **questions are positive signs**. They indicate that investors are interested enough to want to know more. Even challenging questions suggest they're seriously considering your business (otherwise they'd be politely quiet and simply never call you back). Every question gives you an opportunity to reinforce your vision, clarify doubts, and demonstrate your composure under pressure.

"Questions aren't interrogations; they're invitations to deepen the conversation. Each investor question is a door—your answer either walks through it confidently or slams it shut."

Consider Alisha, an entrepreneur who pitched a bold concept: using drones to deliver fresh smoothies in urban areas. During her presentation, Alisha's energy was infectious and her deck was visually stunning. But when it came to Q&A, the angels in the room began asking the hard questions: "How will you navigate regulations for flying drones in populated areas? What about drone battery life during rush hour? Have you conducted any pilot deliveries to test this in an actual neighborhood?"

Alisha, brimming with optimism, had *no solid answers*. She essentially replied, "We'll figure it out as we go; trust me, it'll work!" For many investors, that wasn't sufficient. Half of them declined, saying it was too high-risk with too little validation. A few loved her passion and still invested, but many didn't, precisely because her Q&A revealed gaps in preparation.

Alisha took this as a valuable learning experience. She used the partial funding she did secure to run a pilot program in one neighborhood, gathered actual performance data, and *then* re-approached the hesitant angels with evidence in hand. Seeing concrete results (successful drone deliveries with satisfied customers), the remaining investors enthusiastically came on board.

The lesson? **Enthusiasm must be backed by evidence.** Investor questions often revolve around traction, risks, and contingency plans—and being prepared for those can transform skepticism into support.

Strategies for Mastering the Q&A

How can you expertly navigate the Q&A terrain? Here are proven guidelines:

Listen Attentively and Stay Calm

When a question is asked, listen to it completely. Don't interrupt the person asking, even if you think you know where they're headed.

Sometimes, founders get so eager to respond that they jump in and end up not addressing the investor's true concern.

Take a brief pause after the person finishes—this shows thoughtfulness. If needed, **clarify the question** before answering: "To make sure I understand correctly, you're asking about how we'd scale the infrastructure if demand suddenly surges, correct?" This not only buys you a moment to gather your thoughts but also demonstrates respect for the questioner.

No matter how pointed or skeptical the question, maintain your composure. Keep your body language open (avoid crossing your arms defensively) and your tone measured. Investors are evaluating not just your answers, but how you handle pressure. If you become flustered or defensive, they may worry about how you'll manage the real stresses of building a business. Take a breath, and respond with calm confidence.

Honesty and Humility = Credibility

You won't have a perfect answer to every question—and that's perfectly acceptable. If you genuinely don't know something, it's far better to acknowledge it than to bluff. Say something like, "That's an excellent question. To be candid, that's an area we're still researching. Here's what we **do** know so far, and here's our plan to address that gap..."

Investors appreciate honesty; it builds trust. **Never fabricate** a number or claim on the spot. It's entirely acceptable to say, "I don't have that figure at hand, but I'll follow up with you promptly." Just ensure you actually do follow up later.

Pair humility with ambition: admit what you don't know, but emphasize that you're resourceful and committed to finding the answer or solution. This balance shows both self-awareness and determination—qualities investors value highly.

Prepare for Common Questions

While you can't predict everything investors might ask, many questions are fairly standard. Before any pitch meeting, **brainstorm a list of likely questions** you might receive. Typical ones include:

- How will you acquire customers (marketing strategy)?

- What if a large competitor enters your space?

- What are your customer acquisition costs?

- What keeps you up at night about this business?

- How will you use the investment specifically?

- What's your contingency plan if sales develop more slowly than projected?

Also, if there's any obvious challenge or risk in your business model—*don't avoid it.* In fact, it can be powerful to address a known concern proactively during your pitch: "You might be wondering if drone-delivered smoothies could face regulatory hurdles—we've already initiated conversations with city officials in two districts to establish compliance pathways."

By addressing potential objections yourself, you demonstrate you're not naive to the challenges. But if you haven't already covered it in your presentation, be prepared when it comes up in Q&A.

Investors will probe the toughest parts of your plan—that's their responsibility. Don't take it personally; view it as them saying "Show me this can really work." If you've thought through those challenges, you'll have convincing responses. If you haven't, take notes for improvement.

Keep Answers Clear and Concise

Just as in the pitch itself, rambling in your answers can undermine your credibility. Address each question directly, and avoid tangents. If a yes/no answer is appropriate, start with that, then provide a brief explanation.

For example: Q: "Do you have intellectual property protection?" A: "Yes—we've filed a provisional patent for our core algorithm, and as we gather market feedback, we plan to file a full patent within a year. We're also maintaining certain trade secrets on our matching process."

This is clear and focused. If you receive a multi-part question, it helps to jot down quick notes as the person speaks so you address all components. It's perfectly acceptable to have a notepad for this purpose in a meeting.

Demonstrate Coachability and Grace

Some questions may contain implicit criticism, such as "Don't you think your growth projections are overly optimistic?" or "It seems you have limited experience in this industry—how will you overcome that?" It's natural to feel defensive when faced with such challenges. But a great founder remains **coachable**.

For the projections question, you might respond: "Our projections are indeed ambitious. We believe they're achievable based on X, Y, Z assumptions—however, we understand the future holds uncertainties. We've also modeled a conservative case which still shows a viable business, and I'd be happy to share those numbers."

For the experience question: "That's a fair observation. While I don't have decades in this industry, my background in software gives me a fresh perspective on solving these problems. I've also surrounded myself with advisors who have extensive nonprofit sector experience. I'm a quick learner and completely immersed in understanding the market dynamics. Additionally, coming from outside the industry allows me to approach problems without preconceptions about 'how things have always been done'."

Here you transform a potential weakness into a strength, while acknowledging the legitimate concern. **Every question is an opportunity to reinforce your strengths or address your challenges constructively.**

End on a Positive Note

As the Q&A concludes, thank investors for their thoughtful questions and time. You might sense how the meeting went by their closing remarks ("This sounds promising, we'd like to follow up" versus simply "Thanks for the presentation").

Regardless, maintain professionalism. If time runs short before you can address every question, offer to continue the discussion afterward or via email. Sometimes a question raised toward the end might be crucial; don't rush your answer. If truly pressed for time, note that you'll provide a thorough response as part of your follow-up.

In Alisha's case, once she gathered real data from her test runs, her confidence in Q&A soared. She could answer questions with evidence ("We've completed 50 successful drone deliveries with zero incidents; here's how we addressed the initial regulatory and technical concerns..."). Investors love when you can support answers with numbers or user testimonials. It transforms the conversation from theoretical to tangible.

To summarize: **stay composed, be honest, and view Q&A as a continuation of your pitch by other means.** Even when facing challenging questions, treat them as collaborative problem-solving. Investors ask difficult questions not only to test you but also because they want to identify potential obstacles *before* they invest. Show that you welcome feedback.

If an investor makes a suggestion ("Have you considered targeting corporate sponsors for your volunteer platform as a revenue stream?"), you might respond, "We haven't explored that deeply yet, but that's an intriguing avenue, and we'll definitely investigate it. Thank you." This transforms Q&A from an interrogation into a productive conversation.

One final technique: occasionally you might encounter a question you did prepare for, and you have supporting materials ready. It's appropriate to say, "I have a slide in the appendix that addresses exactly that, if I may show it," and briefly present the visual. This can impress investors, showing you anticipated their concern. Use this sparingly and only when it genuinely enhances your answer.

By handling questions with confidence and thoughtfulness, you demonstrate precisely the qualities that convert an investor's "maybe" into a "yes." They'll conclude, "This founder is the real deal—they understand their business deeply and can navigate whatever challenges arise."

The Funding Landscape: Options and Strategies for Every Stage

Up to this point, we've focused primarily on pitching to angel investors—a common path for early-stage startups. But one size doesn't fit all when it comes to funding. The entrepreneurial journey can be financed in numerous ways, and a savvy founder will consider **multiple funding strategies** to find the optimal fit.

Whether you're just starting out or planning your next growth phase, it's crucial to understand the full menu of options available. In the spirit of Jim Rohn's wisdom, *"Success is neither magical nor mysterious. Success is the natural consequence of consistently applying the basic fundamentals."* One of those fundamentals is knowing your funding options.

Let's explore them, with a motivational framework, so you can choose a path (or combination of paths) that aligns with your vision and values.

1. Bootstrapping (Self-Funding) (continued)

The primary advantage is control—you answer to no one but your customers. Many legendary companies began this way. The challenge, naturally, is that growth can be slower and resources limited, which demands discipline.

Jim Rohn put it perfectly: "We must all suffer one of two pains: the pain of discipline or the pain of regret." In business terms, the bootstrapping entrepreneur chooses the pain of discipline—careful budgeting, frugality, creative problem-solving—but avoids the potential regret of surrendering large equity stakes or accumulating debt prematurely.

"Bootstrapping isn't just a funding strategy—it's a mindset that forces you to build value before valuation. When every dollar is your own, you develop muscles of efficiency that will serve you even in abundance."

Consider Sarah, a college student who launched a small online boutique with just $1,500 of her own money. She stretched every dollar—starting with minimal inventory, creating a simple website, and handling all marketing through free social media channels. Though challenging, she developed extraordinary resourcefulness and efficiency. Her discipline paid off as she eventually generated profit and grew her boutique from that tiny initial investment.

Bootstrapping isn't easy, but it forces you to focus on building a real business that sustains itself. Plus, owning 100% of something you built is tremendously rewarding. If you can manage it, even bootstrapping for a period (until you've validated your concept) puts you in a stronger position when you do approach investors.

2. Friends & Family: Your First Believers

Another common early funding source is the three Fs -- Friends, Family, and Fools (the last F is said with affection, implying people who invest based on their relationship with you rather than rigid analysis). Many entrepreneurs receive their first capital from personal connections who believe in them.

This approach is both powerful and delicate. On one hand, these supporters tend to be more patient and understanding than formal investors. On the other hand, mixing finances with personal relationships requires careful handling. If you accept investment from relatives or friends, always document everything clearly -- how much they contributed, whether it's a loan you'll repay or an equity stake, and any expectations regarding returns or involvement.

For example, Jake convinced his grandmother and cousin to invest in his homemade cookie subscription box venture. Grandma provided $2,000 as a loan, and his cousin contributed $1,000 for a small equity percentage. Jake wisely drafted a simple agreement outlining repayment terms and ownership stakes. This kept expectations clear and family gatherings free from tension.

The key is communication. Treat these arrangements professionally even though they involve your inner circle. And never accept money from someone who can't afford to lose it -- remind family investors that startups carry significant risks. With transparency and mutual respect, friends and family funding can provide both capital and a powerful vote of confidence as you launch your venture.

3. Angel Investors: Smart Money with Wings

We've explored angels extensively, so we'll be concise here. Angel investors are affluent individuals who typically invest $10,000 to $100,000 (sometimes more) each in startups they find promising, usually in exchange for equity.

The true value of angels is in providing smart money: they often contribute expertise and connections alongside capital. Remember Jim Rohn's insight: "You are the average of the five people you spend the most time with." Bringing the right angel onto your team effectively adds a powerhouse to your inner circle.

For instance, Aisha developed an eco-friendly cleaning product. She connected with an angel at a pitch meetup who invested $25,000 and introduced her to a major retailer that later became a key distribution partner. The takeaway: the right angel can elevate your startup exponentially.

Approach angels with the mindset of forming a partnership, not just a transaction. Demonstrate passion backed by preparation, and they could become your mentor and champion on the journey ahead.

4. Venture Capital (VC): Rocket Fuel for Growth

VC funding becomes relevant once you've gained meaningful traction and need substantial capital to scale rapidly. Venture capital firms manage investment funds and make larger investments (from hundreds of thousands to tens of millions of dollars) in exchange for significant equity stakes.

They typically seek high-growth, high-potential startups in technology or innovative sectors. If an angel is like a supportive mentor, a VC is more like a strategic partner with ambitious expectations. Venture capital can be transformative -- like rocket fuel that can propel your business into orbit -- but it comes with the trade-off of diluted ownership and accountability to investors.

"Venture capital isn't just money—it's acceleration with accountability. The capital amplifies your vision, but the clock speeds up and the expectations soar in equal measure."

David built a promising AI-driven education platform. A VC firm offered $500,000 for a 20% stake to help him scale. That investment allowed David to assemble a talented team and expand rapidly, but it also meant he now had investors expecting substantial returns and rapid growth.

It's like transitioning from a sprint to a marathon with additional judges evaluating your performance. Jim Rohn reminds us: "Success is something you attract by the person you become." If you want to attract VC success, you must evolve into the kind of leader who can handle accelerated growth and the heightened expectations that accompany it.

VCs will push you to aim higher, but they'll also provide resources and connections to help you achieve ambitious outcomes (like a major acquisition or IPO). The VC path isn't suitable for every business -- and that's perfectly fine. But if your startup requires rapid scaling and you see an opportunity to capture market share quickly, venture capital could be the catalyst you need.

5. Crowdfunding: The Power of Many

The past decade has unlocked the power of the crowd for startup funding. Crowdfunding primarily comes in two forms:

- Rewards-based (like Kickstarter or Indiegogo, where backers pre-purchase a product or receive perks)

- Equity crowdfunding (platforms like SeedInvest or Republic, where people invest relatively small amounts for actual ownership stakes)

Crowdfunding can be an excellent way to validate your product and raise capital simultaneously. It's also a marketing event -- a successful campaign builds a community of early supporters and advocates.

Consider Mia, a musician who developed an innovative music-learning app. Rather than seeking a single large investor, she launched a crowdfunding campaign with a goal of $10,000 to fund development. She offered backers early access and exclusive content. By creating a compelling video and mobilizing supporters through social media, Mia exceeded her goal and raised $15,000 in just two weeks.

This not only provided the funding she needed but also demonstrated strong market interest in her concept. As Zig Ziglar noted, "People often say that motivation doesn't last. Well, neither does bathing -- that's why we recommend it daily." In crowdfunding, you must continually energize your supporters throughout the campaign -- with updates, appreciation, and new milestones -- to maintain momentum.

The approach requires diligent work, but the rewards extend beyond funding. The caveat: if you promise specific rewards, you must deliver them, which can be challenging for early-stage ventures. With equity crowdfunding, you'll have numerous small investors to keep updated. Despite these considerations, crowdfunding democratizes the investment process -- allowing your customers and supporters to become your investors, creating a powerful alignment of interests.

6. Small Business Loans & Bank Financing: Traditional Capital

Not all businesses fit the high-risk, high-growth model that equity investors seek. If you have a more conventional business (such as a retail store, service company, or manufacturing operation), a small business loan might be the appropriate solution.

Banks and government-backed programs (like SBA loans in the U.S.) can provide funds that you repay with interest while retaining complete ownership of your company. The advantage: you don't surrender equity or control. The challenge: you typically must personally guarantee the loan, and you're obligated to repay it regardless of your business's success, which can create significant pressure if revenue develops slowly.

Carlos planned to open a neighborhood café. He needed $50,000 for equipment and space renovation. With a solid business plan and good credit history, he secured a favorable SBA loan. With the funds in hand, he launched his café, and through attentive management (and excellent coffee), he maintained his repayment schedule while building his dream business.

The disciplined approach required here echoes Jim Rohn's observation: "Discipline is the bridge between goals and accomplishment." Taking on a loan imposes natural discipline -- monthly payments are a powerful motivator to achieve profitability! If you have confidence in your plan and the financials make sense, loans can provide straightforward funding without diluting ownership.

Be conservative in how much you borrow -- avoid overly optimistic projections. And explore programs that might offer advantageous terms (for example, some governments provide special loans for startups, or banks might offer better rates with assets or a cosigner).

7. Grants & Competitions: Non-Dilutive Opportunities

This category is often overlooked but can be invaluable, especially for certain industries or social impact ventures. Grants are non-dilutive funds (meaning you don't sacrifice equity) typically provided by governments, foundations, or institutions to support businesses that meet specific criteria (advancing technology, benefiting communities, etc.).

Startup competitions also belong in this category -- many cities, universities, and corporations host business plan competitions where winners receive cash prizes or resources. The primary benefit of grants and prizes: they represent essentially free money you don't repay or trade for equity. The challenge: they can be highly competitive and often require significant effort in developing applications or proposals.

"A grant is like finding water in the desert—it doesn't ask for equity, interest, or repayment. But like a desert mirage, many chase it while few find it. The secret is persistence and precision in showing how your vision aligns perfectly with the grantor's mission."

For instance, Priya developed a low-cost device helping farmers monitor soil health. Instead of approaching investors, she entered a Tech-for-Good grant competition. After multiple rounds of pitching and demonstrating her product's impact potential, she won a $10,000 grant plus free office space. That funding allowed her to build out her prototype without diluting her ownership.

As Jim Rohn wisely noted, "For every promise, there is a price to pay." The "price" of grant funding is the diligence and effort required to win it, and often the strict reporting or milestones you must satisfy afterward. If you pursue grants, treat the application process as a part-time job to craft a compelling proposal that aligns with the grant's objectives. Similarly, with competitions: prepare your pitch as rigorously as you would for an investor meeting.

Winning can deliver not just funding but also prestige and visibility for your startup.

8. Strategic Partnerships & Corporate Investors: Allies with Resources

Sometimes the funding you need comes attached to a business relationship. Strategic investors are often larger companies in your industry that invest in your startup or form joint ventures because your innovation complements their business. Alternatively, they might become your first major customer, which indirectly funds your growth.

For example, Leo created an innovative fabric made from recycled plastic. A prominent outdoor gear manufacturer recognized potential in using this material for their products. They invested $100,000 in

Leo's startup and established a partnership where they would incorporate his material in their outerwear line.

This arrangement provided Leo not just capital, but also a guaranteed market and credibility through association. In such scenarios, you might give up some equity or exclusivity in certain markets, but you gain a powerful ally. It's like having a big brother in the industry. Such partnerships can dramatically accelerate your growth trajectory (they might provide distribution channels, incorporate your technology into their offerings, etc.).

The caution is to ensure goals remain aligned -- you don't want to become so dependent on one partner that you can't pursue other opportunities. But when structured thoughtfully, strategic funding creates a win-win: the corporate partner achieves innovation through your venture, while you gain resources and reach beyond your current capacity.

Partnerships embody the wisdom that "your network is your net worth." The relationships you cultivate can yield opportunities (and funding) more valuable than money alone.

9. Alternative Financing: Creative Capital Solutions

Beyond traditional loans and equity, there are innovative hybrid models of funding. Microloans are small loans (often a few thousand dollars) typically offered by nonprofit lenders or microfinance institutions, frequently focused on supporting entrepreneurs who can't access conventional bank loans.

They can be invaluable for very small startups or businesses in developing communities. For example, Rosa needed just $2,000 to purchase a used oven and utensils to launch her home catering business. A microloan from a community fund provided that start when no bank would consider her application (due to limited credit history).

By catering weekend events, she repaid the loan within a year and established a thriving small business.

Then there's Revenue-Based Financing (RBF), where an investor or lender provides capital and in return receives a percentage of your monthly revenue until a predetermined amount (typically 1.5-2x the original investment) is repaid. This can be attractive for companies with steady revenues who prefer not to dilute equity or commit to fixed payments regardless of performance.

The repayment flexes with your income -- during slower months you pay less, during stronger months you pay more. This aligns the funder's success with your growth. RBF effectively says, "We succeed when you succeed." A business with subscription revenue or consistent sales might prefer this approach, essentially sharing a portion of future revenue in exchange for immediate capital.

These alternative financing methods usually require that you're already generating revenue (for RBF) or have very modest capital requirements (for microloans). They fill important niches that traditional funding sources might overlook.

The overarching theme is: where there is determination, there is a path to funding. If you have a solid concept and persistence, numerous avenues exist to secure the resources you need. Each requires different approaches -- whether developing a compelling loan application, engaging thousands online, or negotiating a strategic partnership -- but all can lead to the same destination: your venture funded and advancing forward.

This wide array of funding options means entrepreneurs often combine several approaches over time. You might begin by bootstrapping and friends/family support, then bring in angels, and later pursue VC funding or crowdfunding for a major product expansion. There's no universal correct path. The right choice depends on your business model, capital requirements, growth ambitions, and your personal preferences regarding control and risk tolerance.

A moment for reflection: Funding is about more than money -- it's about what accompanies the capital. Each source carries intangible benefits and responsibilities: mentorship, control dynamics, growth expectations, market validation, accountability. When selecting your funding strategy, consider beyond the dollars: what else do I need from my backers?

If you value guidance and experience, angels or established VCs might be ideal. If independence is paramount, bootstrapping or loans could serve you better. If community engagement matters most, crowdfunding shines. The empowering truth is: regardless of how your venture is funded, **you** remain the driving force behind its success. Money can amplify and accelerate, but your vision and execution determine the ultimate outcome. As the founder, you are the constant in any funding equation.

Practically speaking, research thoroughly and speak with entrepreneurs who have used each approach. If you know someone who ran a successful crowdfunding campaign, learn from their experience. If you have a connection who raised venture capital, understand their journey (and perhaps secure an introduction). The more deeply you understand each option, the more strategically you can design your funding roadmap.

Wisdom From the Trenches: Real-World Lessons

Sometimes the most powerful way to synthesize this guidance is through real-world stories of entrepreneurs who've navigated the funding and pitching landscape. Let's examine several inspiring examples that highlight passion, precision, and perseverance -- and the practical lessons you can apply to your own journey.

Lesson 1: The Power of the Right Partner — Rob's SmartHive Success

We met Rob earlier, the beekeeper-turned-tech entrepreneur. His story merits revisiting for its valuable insights. He had developed a niche product -- smart beehive sensors -- and faced skepticism at every turn. But when he finally connected with an angel investor who shared his passion for beekeeping, everything transformed.

That angel provided not just $60,000 in seed funding, but also validation and industry connections. With this support, Rob methodically executed his plan: refining his product and partnering with beekeeping supply stores to reach customers. Within twelve months, SmartHive evolved from a garage concept to being implemented by beekeepers across four countries.

The key lesson here: alignment matters profoundly. When seeking investors, prioritize those who intuitively understand your vision through personal interest or relevant experience. A well-aligned investor can open doors you didn't know existed. Rob often acknowledges that beyond the capital, his angel's guidance on distribution strategies and scaling approaches dramatically accelerated SmartHive's growth.

This underscores that funding relationships extend far beyond transactions -- the right investor partnership can exponentially amplify your success. For you, this means don't simply accept funding from anyone willing to offer it; carefully consider who they are and what else they bring to the table. The right partner can transform a challenging climb into a collaborative journey of growth.

Lesson 2: Evidence Trumps Enthusiasm — Alisha's Drone Delivery Pivot

Alisha's tale of drone-delivered smoothies provided a cautionary example about stumbling during investor Q&A. But it's equally a story about resilience and adaptation. After initially failing to convince all potential angels due to lack of evidence, Alisha didn't abandon her vision.

Instead, she secured smaller initial investment, proved her concept on a limited scale, and then returned to fundraise again -- this time armed with data and a refined pitch. The previously hesitant investors were impressed by her progress and willingness to adapt her approach based on their feedback. Alisha successfully closed the full angel round on her second attempt.

Today, her startup is testing drone deliveries in multiple neighborhoods, systematically addressing regulatory requirements one step at a time. The lesson? Feedback is invaluable, even when it feels like criticism. Those challenging questions that initially tripped her up actually highlighted exactly what she needed to address: conducting a pilot, gathering performance data, and reducing risk factors.

Rather than interpreting investor hesitation as rejection, she viewed it as guidance for improvement. In the entrepreneurial journey, failure only becomes permanent when you stop trying. Alisha's passion for her concept never wavered, but she coupled it with precision in her second approach -- concrete answers, actual metrics, and a more detailed implementation plan. This powerful combination ultimately prevailed.

The takeaway for your journey is to embrace iterative learning. Few founders secure funding on their very first pitch to their first potential investor. You may hear "no" multiple times. Don't be discouraged -- request specific feedback, refine your approach accordingly, and return stronger. Persistence, when informed by continuous learning, becomes nearly unbeatable.

"The strongest founders aren't those who never stumble—they're those who get back up with new wisdom after each fall. Every 'no' is a gift if you're willing to unwrap the lesson inside it."

Lesson 3: Beyond Capital — Rita's AquaGuard Story

In the realm of funding, sometimes the peripheral benefits of an investor significantly outweigh the check they write. Consider Rita, founder of AquaGuard, a startup with a mission to provide water purification in remote regions using solar-powered technology.

Rita secured an angel investor who invested $100,000, but more importantly, had extensive connections with government agencies and international NGOs (non-governmental organizations). This proved invaluable because scaling a water solution often requires collaboration with public authorities and aid organizations.

Through her angel's network, Rita established pilot programs in five different countries, supported by local governments and NGOs, within just two years. AquaGuard's impact expanded exponentially, reaching communities that a small startup would have struggled to access independently.

The lesson from the field: the right funding partner can provide credibility and network access that money alone cannot buy. Rita's experience teaches us to think strategically about investor selection. Sometimes a smaller investment from someone who deeply understands your sector and can actively facilitate growth is more valuable than a larger check from a passive investor.

For entrepreneurs with socially-oriented or complex ventures, this is particularly relevant -- alignment of mission with your investor can create a powerful force multiplier. When evaluating potential investors, always consider their social capital (their relationships, their influence) alongside their financial capital.

Each of these stories -- Rob, Alisha, Rita (and Ava's journey with the pitch deck) -- reinforces a common theme: passion + preparation = progress. Rob's passion for his product connected with an investor prepared to help; Alisha's enthusiasm evolved into methodical preparation; Rita's mission to improve lives was amplified by an investor's extensive network. In the real world of entrepreneurship, neither raw enthusiasm nor pure analysis alone prevails -- it's the synthesis of both.

Another lesson that emerges clearly is the importance of resilience. Every founder encountered obstacles: Rob was told his concept was "too niche," Alisha initially faced rejection from half her audience, Rita tackled enormous bureaucratic challenges. Yet, they persisted. The entrepreneurial path contains many twists and setbacks, but as long as you maintain focus on your mission and learn from each experience, you will find a way forward.

Finally, these field lessons highlight the fundamental nature of the startup ecosystem: it thrives on relationships. Rob found an advocate in his angel; Alisha converted skeptics into supporters; Rita collaborated with governments through her investor's connections. Your journey will inevitably involve others -- mentors, team members, investors, customers. Each relationship can teach you something or create new opportunities.

Cultivate these connections genuinely. Be authentic in sharing your vision and gracious in receiving guidance. When you pitch, you're not merely requesting capital; you're inviting people to join you in a venture that, if successful, benefits everyone involved -- and potentially society at large.

The Next Step: Your Call to Action

You've reached the conclusion of this chapter -- and what a comprehensive journey we've covered: from understanding investor psychology, to crafting compelling pitch materials, delivering with confidence, navigating challenging questions, exploring diverse funding pathways, and learning from real founders' experiences. That's a wealth of actionable wisdom. But knowledge alone doesn't create change -- action does.

Now it's your turn. It's time to transform these insights into tangible steps for your venture. Whether you're still refining your concept or already actively fundraising, commit to moving forward with both passion and precision. Passion will sustain you through challenges and inspire others to rally to your cause. Precision will ensure you complete the necessary preparation, refine your pitch, and execute effectively. When you combine both elements, you become truly formidable.

Here's your call to action, entrepreneur: begin making your plan a reality, today. If you haven't yet, outline that pitch deck -- even as an exercise to clarify your thinking. Identify at least five potential investors or funding sources and research how to approach them. Practice articulating your business concept in one minute, in one sentence, in one paragraph -- you'll need all these versions at different times. Reach out to someone who can provide feedback or an introduction. Each small step builds momentum.

Remember, you don't need everything to be perfect before beginning. As Zig Ziglar wisely noted, "You don't have to be great to start, but you have to start to be great." Take that first step. The path will reveal itself as you progress. The most successful entrepreneurs aren't necessarily those with the most elaborate business plans, but those who are relentless in execution and continuous learning.

"The distance between dreams and reality is called action. Every day you take a step, however small, you shrink that distance until one day your vision and your life become one and the same."

When you enter that investor meeting or launch that crowdfunding campaign, approach it with the mindset that you're not simply asking for money; you're inviting others into a meaningful journey. It's like saying, "I have a vision for something important. With your support, here's what we can achieve together."

One of the most powerful insights from experienced founders is: "Don't just request funding; invite them into the story. Show them you value their expertise, that you have a clear plan for growth, and that together you can build something extraordinary." When you frame it as a partnership rather than a transaction, you transform the dynamic completely -- it's not a plea, it's an opportunity you're sharing.

So, as you step forward to fund and pitch your dream, keep this core message close: Funding and pitching with passion and precision means caring deeply about your mission, preparing thoroughly to achieve it, and boldly engaging those who can help you along the way. You have something special -- a vision that burns within you. Fuel that vision with knowledge, strengthen it with diligent effort, and let it shine through every conversation and presentation.

Take a moment to visualize your success: you standing confidently before investors or supporters, articulately sharing your story. They're engaged, nodding with understanding. They're becoming excited about the future you're creating. And then -- they're committed! Imagine the handshake, the congratulations, the influx of resources to build what you've envisioned. That moment is within reach, but it begins with the steps you take right now.

Let's conclude with one more reflection from Jim Rohn: "Success is neither magical nor mysterious. Success is the natural consequence of consistently applying the basic fundamentals." In this chapter, you've learned the fundamentals of funding and pitching. Apply them consistently -- that is your practical magic. Stay curious, stay persistent, and stay positive. The entrepreneurial path is challenging, but it's also one of the most rewarding journeys you can undertake.

Your vision deserves to become reality. The capital and support you need are out there, waiting for a founder who approaches with authentic passion and well-developed precision. Be that founder.

Now, prepare yourself and move forward. Send that email, make that call, schedule that meeting. Share your vision with the world. The next success story -- the next "garage to greatness" narrative -- could very well be yours. And years from now, you might be the one writing a chapter or giving a presentation, inspiring a new generation of entrepreneurs with your story of how you funded and pitched your way to success.

Go transform your dream into reality -- the world is ready for it, and so are you. The journey of a thousand miles begins with a single step. Take yours today.

8

FINANCIAL FLUENCY — MASTERING THE NUMBERS THAT DRIVE SUCCESS

The Decision That Almost Cost Everything

The conference room fell silent as I placed the bank statement on the table. My co-founder David stared at it, his expression shifting from confusion to alarm. "This can't be right," he whispered, reaching for the document. But we both knew it was. Treydora, our fast-growing startup that had just secured its second round of funding, was hemorrhaging cash at a rate that would leave us bankrupt in less than sixty days.

How did we get here? We had passionate users, a growing team, and investors who believed in our vision. We had mastered product development, marketing, and customer acquisition. But we had neglected the financial foundations that would sustain all of it.

"I thought we had at least six months of runway," David said, the color draining from his face.

"So did I," I admitted. "But we've been tracking projections, not actuals. Our burn rate is nearly double what we planned."

That night, I couldn't sleep. As I paced my living room at 3 AM, a sobering truth crystallized: no matter how brilliant your idea or how devoted your team, *financial mismanagement can kill even the most promising venture.* In that moment of clarity, I made a commitment that would save Treydora and transform how I built businesses thereafter: **I would become as fluent in finance as I was in product and vision.**

The next morning, I called an emergency meeting. "We have a problem," I told our small team. "But more importantly, we have a path forward. We're going to master our finances with the same intensity we've applied to everything else."

What unfolded over the next six weeks was a financial crash course that pulled us back from the brink—and ultimately gave us the foundation to scale sustainably. Today, I'm sharing those hard-won lessons so that you, fellow founder, can build financial fluency from day one rather than in a moment of crisis.

Founder's Truth: "Your brilliant vision can be derailed by financial blindness. The numbers tell a story about your business—learn to read it fluently, or risk having someone else write your ending."

The Language of Business: Understanding Financial Statements

In my journey from healthcare professional to tech entrepreneur, I had to learn that finance isn't just about tracking money—it's about understanding the narrative of your business through numbers. Financial statements are the essential chapters of that story.

Think of financial statements as the vital signs of your business, just as I once monitored the vital signs of patients in the ICU. They reveal the health of your company, highlight potential problems, and guide your decision-making. Let's explore the three critical financial statements every founder needs to understand:

The Income Statement: Your Business Performance Story

An income statement (sometimes called a Profit & Loss or P&L statement) answers a fundamental question: Is your business profitable? It shows revenue, expenses, and the resulting profit or loss over a specific period.

When I first looked at Treydora's income statement during our financial crisis, I realized we had been focusing only on growing top-line revenue without understanding our true costs. Our gross margin (revenue minus direct costs) seemed healthy at 70%, but our operating expenses were consuming that margin and more.

The income statement follows a simple but powerful structure:

- **Revenue** (the money you earn from selling products or services)

- **Less Cost of Goods Sold (COGS)** (direct costs related to producing your offerings)

- **= Gross Profit**

- **Less Operating Expenses** (salaries, rent, marketing, etc.)

- **= Operating Income**

- **Plus/Minus Other Income/Expenses** (interest, taxes, etc.)

- **= Net Income** (the bottom line)

Learning to read this statement properly revealed that while our user acquisition costs appeared reasonable in isolation, they were unsustainable given our current revenue per user. Without this insight, we would have continued an ultimately fatal strategy.

Financial Fluency: "Don't just glance at revenue and profit—understand the journey between them. The path from top line to bottom line reveals opportunities for optimization and threats to your survival."

The Balance Sheet: Your Business Position Story

If the income statement shows how your business performed over time, the balance sheet reveals its financial position at a specific moment. It's a snapshot of what your company owns (assets), owes (liabilities), and the resulting value to owners (equity).

The balance sheet always follows the fundamental accounting equation:

Assets = Liabilities + Equity

When our financial crisis hit, our balance sheet revealed something critically important: while we had cash in the bank from our recent funding, we also had rapidly growing accounts payable (bills we owed but hadn't paid). We were creating financial obligations faster than we were generating resources to meet them.

Here's what to look for on your balance sheet:

- **Assets:** Cash, accounts receivable (money owed to you), inventory, equipment, intellectual property

- **Liabilities:** Accounts payable (bills you owe), loans, credit lines, accrued expenses

- **Equity:** Founder investments, investor capital, retained earnings (accumulated profits)

One powerful metric I learned to calculate from the balance sheet was the **quick ratio** (cash plus accounts receivable divided by current liabilities). This told us how many months we could operate if revenue suddenly stopped—a vital measure for any startup. When I calculated Treydora's quick ratio, it was below 1.0, meaning we couldn't cover our short-term obligations. This was a glaring red flag.

Financial Command: "Your balance sheet is the truth-teller about your business's financial health right now. No amount of future potential can overcome a fundamentally imbalanced equation for long."

The Cash Flow Statement: Your Business Survival Story

The third critical financial document, and perhaps the most important for early-stage companies, is the cash flow statement. It tracks the actual movement of money in and out of your business, answering the essential question: Are we generating or consuming cash?

During Treydora's financial overhaul, the cash flow statement became our guiding star. While the income statement showed us becoming profitable on paper, the cash flow statement revealed we wouldn't survive long enough to see that profitability materialize.

The cash flow statement breaks down into three sections:

- **Operating Activities:** Cash generated or consumed by your core business operations

- **Investing Activities:** Cash used for long-term investments like equipment or received from selling assets

- **Financing Activities:** Cash from loans, investors, or paid out to owners

Studying our cash flow statement, I discovered a critical insight: while we were growing revenue, we were paying expenses immediately but waiting 45-60 days to collect payment from enterprise customers. This timing mismatch was creating a cash crunch even though our business model was fundamentally sound.

Cash Reality: "Profit is an opinion, but cash is a fact. You can't pay employees, rent, or vendors with accounts receivable or paper profits. In the early stages, cash flow management is your lifeline."

Financial Fitness: Creating Systems That Work

Armed with a deeper understanding of financial statements, our next step was to establish robust systems for tracking, analyzing, and acting on our financial data. As an entrepreneur, you need systems that grow with you from day one to IPO.

Starting Right: Early-Stage Financial Tracking

When I launched my first company, I tracked everything in spreadsheets. This worked initially but quickly became unwieldy. By the time we faced our financial crisis at Treydora, we had outgrown our systems without replacing them with something more robust.

For solo founders or small startups, begin with these fundamentals:

1. Separate Personal and Business Finances

Open a dedicated business bank account immediately, even if you're pre-revenue. Use a business credit card for expenses. This separation is non-negotiable—it protects you legally (maintaining your corporate veil) and makes accounting infinitely simpler.

When I started my first venture, I made the rookie mistake of mixing personal and business expenses. During tax season, I spent agonizing hours trying to reconstruct which expenses belonged to the business. Never again.

2. Choose Accounting Software That Scales

Even if you're a solo founder with minimal transactions, invest in proper accounting software from day one. QuickBooks, Xero, and FreshBooks are popular options that grow with your business.

At Treydora, we started with Wave (free for basic accounting) and later migrated to QuickBooks as we scaled. The platform you choose matters less than establishing the habit of proper financial recording.

3. Set Up a Chart of Accounts That Makes Sense

Your chart of accounts is the organizational system for categorizing financial transactions. Create categories that align with your business model and give you meaningful insights.

For example, rather than a single "Marketing" category, we created sub-categories for digital ads, content creation, and events. This granularity later helped us identify which marketing investments yielded the highest returns.

4. Establish Regular Financial Rituals

Make financial review a consistent habit:

- **Daily:** Check cash balances

- **Weekly:** Review pending payments and upcoming expenses

- **Monthly:** Complete reconciliation and review financial statements

- **Quarterly:** Conduct deeper analysis and adjust forecasts

During our financial overhaul at Treydora, we instituted "Financial Fridays"—a sacred two-hour block when our leadership team reviewed key metrics and made necessary adjustments. This ritual helped us avoid future surprises and build financial awareness throughout the organization.

Financial Discipline: "The most successful founders aren't necessarily financial experts—they're disciplined enough to establish systems and rituals that keep financial reality front and center."

Growing Stronger: Mid-Stage Financial Management

As your company grows, your financial systems must evolve. When Treydora expanded beyond 20 employees and $1 million in annual revenue, we implemented these next-level practices:

1. Develop a Financial Dashboard

Create a dashboard of 5-7 key financial metrics specific to your business model. For Treydora, these included:

- Monthly recurring revenue (MRR)

- Customer acquisition cost (CAC)

- Customer lifetime value (LTV)

- Burn rate

- Runway (months of cash remaining)

- Gross margin percentage

- Net revenue retention

This dashboard became our compass, displayed prominently in our office and reviewed in every leadership meeting. It eliminated financial blindspots and aligned our team around the metrics that mattered most.

2. Implement Financial Controls

As you scale, establish policies for spending, approvals, and financial oversight. These aren't bureaucratic obstacles—they're guardrails that prevent costly mistakes.

After our financial wake-up call, we implemented:

- Spending thresholds requiring different levels of approval

- Monthly budget-to-actual reviews for each department

- Quarterly forecast updates

- Clear ownership of financial outcomes (not just activities)

3. Consider Fractional Financial Leadership

Before you can afford a full-time CFO, consider hiring a fractional CFO or financial consultant. This experienced professional can help establish mature financial processes, prepare for fundraising, and provide strategic financial guidance.

This was a game-changer for Treydora. Our fractional CFO, Ellen, worked just 10 hours per week but transformed our financial operations. She helped us restructure payment terms with customers, optimize our pricing model, and build a financial forecast that actually predicted our future with reasonable accuracy.

Financial Evolution: "As your company grows, your financial systems must evolve from tracking what happened to predicting what will happen—and providing clear guidance on what should happen next."

The Entrepreneur's Budget: Planning for Success and Survival

Perhaps the most powerful financial tool in your arsenal is a well-constructed budget. A budget isn't a bureaucratic exercise or a wishful projection—it's a strategic roadmap that translates your business vision into financial terms.

The Zero-Based Budgeting Approach

When we restructured Treydora's finances, we adopted zero-based budgeting, a method where you start from zero and justify every expense. Unlike traditional budgeting (which often starts with last year's numbers), zero-based budgeting forces you to question every assumption.

The process works like this:

1. Start with your revenue projections (be conservative)

2. Determine the absolutely essential expenses to generate that revenue

3. Align additional investments with strategic priorities

4. Create contingency plans for different scenarios

Using this approach, we discovered that nearly 30% of our expenses weren't directly contributing to our core growth objectives. We didn't eliminate all of these—some supported our culture or long-term innovation—but we reduced or restructured many to extend our runway.

Budget Reality: "A budget is a conscious choice about how to allocate limited resources for maximum impact. Without one, you're essentially deciding that everything is equally important—which means nothing truly is."

The 50/30/20 Rule for Startups

One framework that helped us regain control was adapting the personal finance 50/30/20 rule for our business:

- **50% on Core Operations** – Activities directly generating revenue or delivering your product/service

- **30% on Growth Initiatives** – Marketing, sales, and product development that expand your market

- **20% on Infrastructure & Innovation** – Systems, culture, and forward-looking investments

This simple framework forced us to prioritize and maintain balance. Before implementing it, we discovered we were spending over 50% on growth alone—an unsustainable approach given our cash position.

Three Scenarios: Plan for Different Futures

Another valuable practice we implemented was developing three budget scenarios:

- **Conservative Case** (70% confidence) – The results you're reasonably certain you can achieve

- **Target Case** (50% confidence) – Your actual goals if things go according to plan

- **Stretch Case** (30% confidence) – What's possible if several things go better than expected

We managed expenses based on the conservative case, set team goals based on the target case, and created incentives around the stretch case. This balanced prudence with ambition.

Most importantly, we created trigger points for adjusting our plans. If we hit 80% of targets for two consecutive months, we would implement specific cost-reduction measures. This removed emotion from difficult decisions by establishing clear thresholds in advance.

Strategic Planning: "The most valuable aspect of budgeting isn't the final numbers—it's the strategic thinking required to produce them. A thoughtful budget forces you to articulate exactly how you'll transform capital into growth."

The Entrepreneur's Financial Tool Kit

Building financial fluency requires the right tools. Here are the solutions that saved Treydora and continue to serve founders at every stage:

Essential Financial Software

1. Accounting Systems

After evaluating several options, we selected **QuickBooks Online** for Treydora because it offered the right balance of usability and sophistication. Other excellent options include:

- **Xero** – Known for its clean interface and strong integration capabilities

- **FreshBooks** – Especially good for service-based businesses with simple needs

- **NetSuite** – For larger organizations requiring enterprise-grade features

Regardless of which platform you choose, look for these critical capabilities:

- Bank feed integration for automatic transaction import

- Cloud-based access for your team and advisors

- Reporting flexibility to create custom financial views

- Integration with your other business systems

2. Forecasting and Modeling Tools

Your accounting system tells you where you've been, but you need forecasting tools to see where you're going. We found these solutions invaluable:

- **Float** – For cash flow forecasting and scenario planning

- **Fathom** – For financial analysis and performance tracking

- **Adaptive Planning** – For more sophisticated budgeting as you scale

For earlier stages, well-structured spreadsheets can work effectively. We created a financial model template that has guided multiple startups through their early growth phases.

3. Billing and Accounts Receivable Management

One revelation from our financial crisis was that we needed to better manage the timing of customer payments. These tools helped us optimize our cash conversion cycle:

- **Stripe** – For payment processing with automation capabilities

- **Bill.com** – For managing both payables and receivables

- **Chargify** – For subscription management and recurring billing

By implementing automated billing reminders and incentives for early payment, we reduced our average collection time from 47 days to 23 days—nearly doubling our available operating cash.

Tool Selection: "Choose financial tools that reduce friction in healthy financial habits. The best system isn't the most powerful—it's the one you'll actually use consistently."

Building Your Financial Dream Team

Even the best tools require the right people to use them effectively. As you grow, consider building your financial team in this sequence:

1. Bookkeeper (Part-time, then full-time)

A skilled bookkeeper maintains accurate financial records and ensures transactions are properly categorized. We started with a part-time bookkeeper who worked just 10 hours per month, then expanded to full-time as transaction volume increased.

2. Accountant (Fractional, then in-house)

An accountant helps with more complex financial matters, including tax planning and financial statement preparation. We worked with an outsourced accounting firm until we reached about $5 million in annual revenue, then brought the function in-house.

3. Financial Analyst (Project-based, then full-time)

A financial analyst helps turn raw financial data into actionable insights. Initially, I performed this role myself with guidance from mentors. Later, we hired an analyst to build more sophisticated models and conduct deeper analyses.

4. CFO (Fractional, then full-time)

A Chief Financial Officer provides strategic financial leadership. As mentioned earlier, our fractional CFO provided tremendous value before we could justify a full-time executive.

Team Building: "Your financial team isn't just about compliance—it's about creating the insights that drive better business decisions. Invest in financial talent before you think you need it."

The Entrepreneur's Financial Mindset

Beyond tools and team members, financial fluency requires developing a particular mindset—one that balances detail-orientation with strategic thinking, conservatism with ambition.

The Paranoid Optimist

I describe the ideal financial mindset for entrepreneurs as "paranoid optimism"—the capacity to simultaneously believe in your vision while maintaining healthy skepticism about projections.

After our financial crisis, I adopted a simple mantra: "Hope for the best, plan for the struggle, and measure relentlessly." This meant:

- Setting ambitious goals aligned with our vision

- Creating contingency plans for when things inevitably deviate from projections

- Establishing clear metrics to track progress and trigger course corrections

This balanced mindset prevents both naive optimism (which can lead to financial disaster) and excessive conservatism (which can limit growth potential).

Financial Paradox: "The entrepreneur's financial mindset contains multitudes: aggressive growth targets balanced by conservative cash management, long-term vision guided by short-term metrics, and confidence in the future paired with clear-eyed assessment of the present."

The Weekly Financial Question Ritual

One practice that transformed my financial leadership was establishing a weekly ritual of financial self-questioning. Every Monday morning, I would ask myself:

1. Do I know our current cash position and runway?

2. Have we received the payments we expected last week?

3. Are there any unusual expenses or financial surprises emerging?

4. Is our actual performance aligning with our forecasts?

5. What financial decision do I need to make this week?

This simple ritual kept financial reality front-of-mind and prevented small issues from becoming major problems. When our team leaders adopted similar practices, our collective financial intelligence multiplied.

The Investor's Perspective

A breakthrough in my financial understanding came from regularly viewing our finances through the eyes of a potential investor. This meant asking:

- Is our business model demonstrably working (with metrics to prove it)?

- Are we efficiently converting capital into growth?

- Is our financial story coherent and compelling?

- Do our financial metrics support our valuation expectations?

This perspective helped us identify and address potential concerns before they were raised by actual investors. When we later entered fundraising discussions, our financial house was in order—giving us a stronger negotiating position and ultimately better terms.

Perspective Shift: "Looking at your finances through others' eyes—investors, customers, team members—reveals blind spots you can't see from your position as a founder. Regularly shift your perspective to gain complete financial awareness."

Financial Crisis Management: Surviving and Thriving

Sometimes, despite your best efforts, financial challenges arise. The difference between companies that survive crises and those that don't often comes down to how quickly they recognize and address financial reality.

The Warning Signs

Through painful experience, I've learned to recognize these early warning signs of financial trouble:

1. **Consistently missing financial projections** – One month might be an anomaly; three consecutive months is a pattern

2. **Declining unit economics** – When the cost to acquire and serve customers rises while revenue per customer remains flat or decreases

3. **Extending payables while accelerating discounts** – Delaying payments to vendors while offering aggressive discounts to accelerate customer payments

4. **Growing faster than cash flow can support** – When increasing sales actually worsens your cash position

5. **Team members expressing financial concerns** – When employees start asking questions about financial stability

When we noticed several of these indicators at Treydora, we initiated our financial overhaul. Had we waited even a month longer, our options would have been far more limited.

Crisis Detection: "Financial crises rarely appear suddenly—they emerge gradually through subtle signals. Train yourself to recognize these warnings while you still have time and options to respond effectively."

The Financial Turnaround Playbook

When facing financial challenges, follow this proven playbook that guided Treydora's recovery:

1. Get Absolute Clarity

First, gather complete and accurate financial information. We conducted a comprehensive financial review, including:

- A detailed cash flow analysis showing weekly projections

- An honest assessment of our true burn rate

- A complete inventory of financial obligations and commitments

- A clear calculation of our remaining runway

2. Communicate Transparently

Share the situation with key stakeholders. We held candid conversations with:

- Our board and investors, presenting both the challenge and our response plan

- Key team members who would be critical to the turnaround

- Essential vendors and partners whose support we needed

The transparency actually strengthened relationships rather than damaging them. As one investor told me, "I'm not upset about the problem; I'm impressed by how you're handling it."

3. Take Decisive Action

Implement immediate measures to extend runway while preserving core capabilities:

- Renegotiate payment terms with vendors (many agreed to 60-90 day terms)

- Adjust pricing strategy to improve cash flow (we introduced annual payment incentives)

- Reduce non-essential expenses (we cut our burn rate by 42% in six weeks)

- Restructure team around essential functions (we reorganized rather than simply cutting)

4. Build Sustainable Solutions

Finally, establish systems to prevent future crises:

- Implement rigorous financial forecasting and monitoring

- Create clear accountability for financial outcomes

- Develop leading indicators that predict potential issues

- Build a culture of financial awareness throughout the organization

Recovery Framework: "Financial recovery requires equal measures of honesty, urgency, and methodical rebuilding. Face reality immediately, act decisively, and then create systems to ensure the situation never repeats."

From Survival to Strategic Finance

The transformation at Treydora didn't end with survival. Once we established sound financial fundamentals, we began using finance as a strategic tool to accelerate growth and create competitive advantages.

Strategic Pricing

We conducted a comprehensive pricing analysis that revealed we were significantly undercharging for our enterprise solution. By implementing value-based pricing, we increased our average contract value by 68% while actually improving our close rate—customers perceived greater value in our higher-priced offering.

Unit Economics Optimization

We obsessively analyzed and improved our unit economics—the fundamental financial relationship between what it costs to acquire and serve a customer versus the revenue they generate.

By understanding these metrics at a granular level, we identified specific customer segments that were significantly more profitable than others. Focusing our marketing efforts on these segments improved overall margins while reducing customer acquisition costs.

Financial Storytelling

Perhaps most importantly, we learned to articulate our business through financial storytelling—explaining how our current metrics connected to our future vision.

When we later raised our Series B round, investors commented that our financial presentation was unusually compelling. One VC partner noted, "You've connected your mission to your metrics in a way that makes your growth feel inevitable rather than aspirational."

Strategic Evolution: "When you move from financial survival to financial strategy, you transform numbers from constraints into competitive advantages. Financial fluency becomes a superpower that accelerates everything else in your business."

Valuing Your Company: The Art and Science of Business Valuation

One of the most consequential financial skills for any founder is the ability to determine what your company is actually worth. During Treydora's growth journey, we faced this question multiple times: when raising capital, when considering acquisition offers, and when issuing equity to key team members.

I discovered that business valuation is equal parts science (analyzing metrics and financials) and art (telling a compelling story about future potential). Let me share what I learned about valuing your venture at different stages.

Why Valuation Matters

Accurate business valuation serves several critical purposes:

- It helps you raise capital at fair terms (without giving away too much equity or overvaluing your company)

- It establishes a framework for employee equity compensation

- It provides a benchmark for measuring growth over time

- It offers clarity when considering potential exits or acquisitions

The most painful valuation lesson I learned came during our first funding round. Without a clear methodology, we accepted a valuation that significantly undervalued our potential. We left millions of dollars of founder equity on the table—a mistake I vowed never to repeat.

Valuation Methods for Different Stages

The appropriate valuation method depends largely on your company's stage. Here's a practical guide to the most relevant approaches at each phase:

Early-Stage Startups (Pre-Revenue or Early Revenue)
1. **Comparable Transaction Method**

When Treydora was just getting started, we examined recent funding rounds for similar companies in our space. By analyzing these "comps," we established a reasonable valuation range.

The process works like this:

- Identify 5-10 companies at similar stages in related industries

- Research their funding amounts and the equity percentages they sold

- Calculate the implied valuations

- Adjust based on your specific differentiators (team strength, technology, traction)

For example, if similar early-stage edtech companies were raising $1 million for 15-20% equity, this implied valuations of $5-6.7 million. We could then adjust this range based on our unique advantages or challenges.

1. **The Berkus Method**

Named after angel investor Dave Berkus, this approach assigns value to five key startup elements:

- Sound idea/concept: $1-2 million

- Prototype/technology: $1-2 million

- Quality team: $1-2 million

- Strategic relationships: $1-2 million

- Product rollout or sales: $1-2 million

Using this method for Treydora, we scored ourselves honestly on each dimension. We had a proven concept and working prototype (high scores), but were still developing strategic relationships (lower score). This gave us a baseline pre-money valuation of approximately $5 million when pitching to early investors.

1. **Risk Factor Summation Method**

This approach starts with a base valuation (often derived from comparable transactions) and then adjusts it by scoring your company across 12 risk factors:

- Management risk

- Stage of business

- Legal/regulatory risk

- Manufacturing risk

- Sales and marketing risk

- Funding risk

- Competition risk

- Technology risk

- Litigation risk

- International risk

- Reputation risk

- Potential lucrative exit

Each factor is rated from -5 (very negative) to +5 (very positive), with each point representing $250,000-$500,000 in valuation adjustment.

We found this method particularly useful because it forced us to confront our weaknesses while also highlighting our strengths. The structured approach also proved persuasive with sophisticated angel investors.

Growth-Stage Companies (Established Revenue)
1. Multiple of Revenue

As Treydora established consistent revenue, we shifted to revenue-based valuation methods. Different industries have different standard multiples, but SaaS companies like ours typically valued at:

- 1-3x ARR (Annual Recurring Revenue) for early-stage

- 4-6x ARR for growth-stage with good metrics

- 7-10x+ ARR for companies with exceptional growth and unit economics

We tracked industry-specific multiples quarterly, as these benchmarks fluctuate with market conditions. During bullish periods for tech, multiples expanded significantly, while during downturns, they contracted.

1. Discounted Cash Flow (DCF)

As our financial forecasting became more sophisticated, we implemented DCF analysis. This method:

- Projects your future cash flows for 3-5 years

- Applies a discount rate to account for the time value of money and risk

- Adds a terminal value representing the business's worth beyond the projection period

- Sums these values to determine present value

The formula looks intimidating at first: Value = $CF_1/(1+r)^1$ + $CF_2/(1+r)^2$ + ... + $CF_n/(1+r)^n$ + $TV/(1+r)^n$

Where:

- CF = Cash flow in the given year

- r = Discount rate

- TV = Terminal value

- n = Number of periods

For early-stage companies, the discount rate is typically high (30-50%) to reflect risk, while later-stage companies might use lower rates (20-30%).

While DCF required significant financial modeling expertise (we eventually hired a financial analyst to build and maintain these models), it provided the most comprehensive view of our company's intrinsic value based on expected future performance.

1. Multiple of EBITDA

As we approached profitability, EBITDA multiples became increasingly relevant. This method simply multiplies your Earnings Before Interest, Taxes, Depreciation, and Amortization by an industry-appropriate multiple.

For software companies, these multiples typically range from 10-20x, depending on growth rate, market position, and overall market conditions.

Strategic Value Factors

Beyond these traditional valuation methods, we learned to articulate strategic value factors that could justify premium valuations:

- **Intellectual Property** – Patents, proprietary technology, or unique methods

- **Market Position** – Industry leadership or rapid market share growth

- **Network Effects** – Built-in advantages that strengthen with scale

- **Growth Rate** – Exceptional growth compared to industry averages

- **Team** – Unique expertise or background of key team members

When preparing for our Series B round, we specifically highlighted our proprietary algorithm and exceptional retention metrics as justification for a higher-than-average multiple.

Valuation Insight: "Your company's worth isn't just what the spreadsheet says today—it's what a compelling vision, supported by current metrics, suggests about tomorrow. Learn to balance numerical analysis with narrative to achieve fair valuation."

Creating a Valuation Framework

Rather than relying on a single method, we developed a valuation framework that incorporated multiple approaches:

1. Calculate valuations using 2-3 methods appropriate for your

stage

2. Create a valuation range rather than a single number

3. Adjust based on current market conditions and investor sentiment

4. Prepare detailed justification for your valuation (the "why" behind the numbers)

5. Understand your BATNA (Best Alternative To a Negotiated Agreement)

This framework provided confidence during fundraising and M&A discussions. Instead of accepting others' valuations, we came prepared with well-reasoned analyses and supporting evidence.

When an acquirer approached us with an offer that significantly undervalued Treydora based on our framework, we confidently declined—a decision that proved wise when we received a substantially better offer six months later.

Practical Valuation Tools

Several tools helped us develop and refine our valuations:

- **Spreadsheet Templates** – We created modular templates for different valuation methods

- **AngelList and Crunchbase** – For researching comparable company valuations

- **Industry Reports** – To stay current on valuation multiples and trends

- **Investor Updates** – Publicly available letters from VCs about market conditions

- **Financial Modeling Software** – For more sophisticated DCF analysis

While these tools provided structure, the most valuable resource was often conversations with other founders who had recently raised capital. These peer insights helped us understand the "real" valuations in our space, beyond what was publicly reported.

Valuation Truth: "Your company is ultimately worth what someone is willing to pay for it. But by mastering valuation methodologies, you enter these negotiations with clarity, confidence, and leverage rather than simply accepting others' assessments."

Your Financial Journey Begins Now

As I reflect on Treydora's financial journey—from near-disaster to strategic strength—I'm reminded of a simple truth: financial fluency isn't innate; it's developed through deliberate practice and learning from both mistakes and successes.

You don't need an accounting degree or Wall Street experience to master entrepreneurial finance. You simply need:

1. **Curiosity** – Ask questions until you truly understand your numbers

2. **Discipline** – Establish and maintain sound financial habits

3. **Perspective** – View finances as a strategic tool, not just a scorekeeping system

4. **Humility** – Recognize what you don't know and seek expertise when needed

My own financial education came through crisis—a painful but effective teacher. You have the opportunity to learn more gradually and systematically.

Start where you are. If you're just launching, begin with the fundamental systems described earlier. If you're already generating revenue, assess your current financial practices against the frameworks shared here. Identify your biggest gap and focus there first.

Remember that financial mastery, like any entrepreneurial skill, develops progressively. Each step you take builds capability and confidence for the next.

"Financial fluency isn't about becoming an accountant—it's about developing the numerical intuition that lets you instantly translate business situations into financial terms and financial reports into strategic insights." — Original

The financial awakening that saved Treydora ultimately transformed my approach to entrepreneurship. I went from seeing finance as a necessary administrative function to recognizing it as the underlying operating system for business success.

Today, I still maintain the daily and weekly financial rituals developed during our turnaround. They've become second nature—as essential to my entrepreneurial practice as customer interviews or product development.

As you continue your founder's journey, embrace the power of financial fluency. Let the numbers tell their story. Learn their language fluently. And use that knowledge to write a business story of sustainable success and impact.

Your most important financial decision isn't in the past or the future—it's what you choose to do right now with the insights you've gained. Take that first step toward financial mastery today. Your business deserves nothing less.

In the next chapter, we'll explore how to leverage artificial intelligence to accelerate every aspect of your startup's growth, from ideation to execution.

9

ACCELERATE WITH INTELLIGENCE — HARNESSING AI FOR STARTUP GROWTH

The New Entrepreneurial Advantage

In the modern startup landscape, artificial intelligence (AI) has evolved from futuristic concept to essential entrepreneurial ally. Think of AI not as a mere tool but as a new class of cognitive material—like discovering that besides wood, metal, and plastic, you can now build with a substance that thinks, learns, and improves itself continuously.

This cognitive material can be shaped into countless forms: a tireless employee who handles repetitive tasks without complaint, a brilliant analyst who processes information at superhuman speed, a creative collaborator who generates fresh perspectives at 3 AM when your own mind has reached its limits. Unlike traditional resources that deplete as you use them, this material actually becomes more valuable with use, learning your preferences and adapting to your specific needs.

It's no longer a luxury reserved for tech giants with massive R&D budgets; it's a practical toolkit available to every founder willing to embrace it. In fact, over three-quarters of businesses today leverage AI in at least one function of their operations.

"The modern founder's unfair advantage isn't just access to AI—it's the courage to reimagine every business function through the lens of intelligence amplification. When others ask 'Can AI help with this specific task?' the visionary asks 'How would this entire process transform if intelligence were unlimited?'"

Remember this fundamental truth as we proceed: **AI isn't here to replace your vision—it's here to amplify it**. The magic happens at the intersection of human ingenuity and artificial intelligence, where your entrepreneurial spark ignites a new realm of possibilities.

The ARISE Method: Implementing AI Across Your Startup

After helping dozens of founders integrate AI into their operations, I've developed a systematic approach I call the ARISE Method—a practical sequence that maximizes AI impact while minimizing disruption:

1. Audit - Conduct a comprehensive review of your current operations, identifying processes that are repetitive, time-consuming, or require significant analysis.

2. Rank - Prioritize potential AI implementations based on three factors: immediate time savings, complexity of implementation, and strategic importance.

3. Implement - Start with one high-impact, low-complexity application to build confidence and demonstrate value to your team.

4. Scale - Expand successful implementations across departments, creating AI champions who can guide adoption within their teams.

5. Evolve - Continuously refine your AI systems based on feedback and results, measuring impact through concrete metrics that matter to your business.

This structured approach prevents the common mistake of over-whelming your team with too many changes simultaneously while ensuring you capture meaningful value at each stage of implementation.

The Founder's AI Creativity Matrix

When it comes to generating breakthrough ideas, AI can function across multiple dimensions. I've found it helpful to visualize this as what I call the "Founder's AI Creativity Matrix"—a powerful model for understanding how to leverage AI for maximum creative output:

Dimension 1: Idea Initiation vs. Refinement

- *Initiation Mode*: Here, you provide minimal guidance and ask AI to generate completely new concepts. Try prompts like "Generate 10 innovative business models for sustainable transportation" or "What are unexplored applications of blockchain in healthcare?"

- *Refinement Mode*: Here, you bring your partial idea and use AI to develop it further. "I have a concept for an app that helps people build daily habits. What features would differentiate it from existing solutions?" or "Help me identify potential weaknesses in this business model."

Dimension 2: Divergent vs. Convergent Thinking

- *Divergent Tools*: These AI applications help you explore widely—expanding possibilities and considering unlikely connections. ChatGPT excels here when you prompt it to "think outside the box" or "combine unlikely elements."

- *Convergent Tools*: These help you narrow and focus—taking broad concepts and refining them into actionable plans. Ask AI to "prioritize these ideas based on feasibility and market size" or "create a decision matrix for selecting the optimal approach."

By consciously moving through different quadrants of this matrix—sometimes seeking wild expansion of possibilities, other times asking for critical analysis and focus—you create a dynamic creativity system that prevents both tunnel vision and endless ideation without execution.

As **Zig Ziglar** famously said, **"You don't have to be great to start, but you have to start to be great,"** and AI ensures you *always have somewhere to start*—no more blank page paralysis.

ChatGPT has emerged as the quintessential partner for idea generation. Think of it as an infinitely patient sounding board with knowledge spanning virtually every industry and domain. Struggling to articulate your unique value proposition or develop a memorable product name? Simply initiate a conversation with ChatGPT and watch the possibilities unfold.

Try prompts like, *"What are five innovative business models in the sustainable transportation space?"* or *"Generate 10 compelling names for a productivity app aimed at creative professionals."* You'll receive a cascade of possibilities to consider and refine.

Many founders use ChatGPT not only to generate initial concepts, but to *expand on promising ideas*, exploring "what-if" scenarios and identifying potential blind spots or challenges. It's like brainstorming on steroids—*brainstorming with intelligence*.

Other AI tools can broaden your perspective in complementary ways. **Notion AI**, integrated seamlessly into the popular Notion workspace, helps outline business plans or product concepts with remarkable clarity. You can input a rough idea and ask the AI to elaborate or structure those thoughts into a coherent framework. It's like having a mentor who helps organize your chaotic inspiration into actionable strategies.

Jasper and **Copy.ai** are specialized AI writing assistants that entrepreneurs use to **generate taglines, mission statements, or even draft emails** when creative wells run dry. They can produce numerous variations of messaging or value propositions, allowing you to select what resonates most powerfully with your vision.

Let's say you have a preliminary concept for addressing a common problem—perhaps an app that helps people build consistent daily habits. An AI tool can help you **conduct rapid market research** by analyzing trends: ask *"What are the most common complaints about existing habit tracker apps?"* and it might synthesize recurring pain points from across reviews and forums. It can even help identify market gaps by assessing existing solutions. In minutes, you could gain insight that might otherwise require days of manual research.

This means from the *earliest stages* of your venture, you're moving with both speed and intelligence.

"AI doesn't replace the entrepreneur's vision—it magnifies it. The founder who truly understands this doesn't waste time asking 'Will AI take my job?' but instead asks 'How can AI help me create jobs that didn't exist before, solving problems we couldn't previously address?'"

From Concept to Creation: Building With AI

Once you've solidified your idea, the next challenge is building it—creating a **Minimum Viable Product (MVP)** or prototype, and then developing it into a full-fledged offering. This phase can be daunting, especially if you're a solo founder or lack specific technical expertise. But here's the empowering truth: *AI can level the playing field dramatically.*

It's like having an on-demand engineering team, design studio, and product consultant all rolled into one. Management guru **Peter Drucker** offered this prescient warning: **"The enterprise that does not innovate ages and declines... and in a period of rapid change such as the present, the decline will be fast."** By building with AI, you're choosing to innovate rapidly and consistently, ensuring your startup remains vibrant and ahead of the curve.

AI in Coding and Development

If you're not a developer, tools like **ChatGPT** (particularly with its advanced GPT-4 model) or **GitHub Copilot** can transform ideas into functional code. Non-technical founders increasingly use ChatGPT to generate code snippets or algorithms by simply describing desired functionality.

For example, *"How can I build a simple website signup form that captures email addresses and stores them in a database?"* will yield step-by-step guidance or even working code samples. This has empowered founders to create initial versions of applications without hiring developers upfront.

A compelling example is **Josh Mohrer**, founder of the audio-note app *Wave*. Josh wasn't a software engineer—he admits experiencing "engineer envy" due to his limited coding knowledge—but he leveraged ChatGPT to **fill his knowledge gaps and write substantial portions of his app's code**. With AI "getting him the rest of the way there," he built Wave essentially solo, and today that application is transcribing and summarizing **over 6,000 hours of audio daily for more than 22,000 subscribers**.

AI enabled a non-technical founder to create a technology product serving thousands—a feat that would have been prohibitively expensive and complicated just a few years ago.

Even if you *are* a developer or have a technical team, AI accelerates your progress exponentially. **GitHub Copilot**, an AI pair-programmer trained on billions of code lines, can autocomplete functions or suggest solutions as you write code. This not only speeds development but also reduces errors by flagging issues or offering improvements in real-time.

As a founder, faster development cycles mean you can iterate your product rapidly, respond to user feedback promptly, and outpace competitors decisively. In the startup world, **speed of execution** often determines whether you lead the market or struggle to catch up. AI provides that crucial acceleration.

Design and Prototyping

Building an MVP encompasses more than coding; it involves design, user experience, and sometimes hardware or physical product development. AI excels here as well. Tools like **Uizard** or **Figma's AI plugins** can transform hand-drawn sketches into functional app mockups. There are AI services where you can request, *"Design a modern e-commerce homepage optimized for conversion,"* and receive professional layout options to refine.

For logos or graphics, generative AI models have revolutionized visual creation—you can generate unique logo concepts or illustrations by describing what you envision. **Runway ML** helps generate and edit images and even videos. Imagine creating a promotional **demo video** of your product without a production team: with Runway, you could generate custom graphics, remove video backgrounds, or add professional effects using simple AI commands.

Some startups use **Lumen5** to automatically transform blog posts or text content into polished videos—invaluable if your MVP needs an explainer video or you want to demonstrate your product with minimal resources.

From MVP to Product Refinement

Once your initial version launches, AI continues to enhance testing and iteration. AI-driven testing tools can automatically identify bugs or security vulnerabilities in your code. Even ChatGPT can **simulate user interactions**—ask it to critique your app's flow ("What might confuse a first-time user during this onboarding process?") and it will highlight potential improvements or confusing elements.

It's like having an unbiased advisor providing feedback at any hour. Some founders even use AI to generate test data or simulated user feedback, helping them prepare for various scenarios before actual users engage with the product.

Consider the **development mindset** with AI as **Steve Jobs** described our relationship with technology: *"What a computer is to me is the most remarkable tool we've ever come up with. It's the equivalent of a bicycle for our minds."* If computers are mental bicycles, **AI is a rocket**. It allows a solo founder to accomplish what once required entire teams. But remember, *you* determine the destination. AI will accelerate your journey, but you must steer the course.

As you build, keep your users' needs in clear focus. AI will handle much of the heavy lifting in creation and iteration, freeing you to concentrate on the *vision* and *experience* you want to deliver.

"The greatest founders don't fear being replaced by AI—they embrace being enhanced by it. They understand that technology doesn't diminish human creativity; it amplifies it beyond what was previously possible."

*"Don't be intimidated by what you can't yet do—be excited by what you **can achieve with AI's assistance**. In building your startup, think of AI as a co-founder with superpowers: it never sleeps, never tires, and stands ready to prototype, code, and create alongside you. Together, there are few limits to what you can accomplish."*

Use AI in your building phase to **prototype rapidly, test continuously, and polish relentlessly.** The faster you can develop a working product, the sooner you'll receive genuine feedback and iterate toward excellence. Historically, a vast gulf separated great ideas from tangible products—AI has dramatically narrowed that gap. Seize this advantage. Build boldly, build quickly, and refine persistently.

The TEAM Framework: AI-Enhanced People Operations

A startup's success isn't determined solely by its product or concept—it's equally shaped by the **people** behind the vision. *Attracting and nurturing an exceptional team* is a paramount priority for any founder. Fortunately, AI can assist here too, ensuring you spend more time with people and less on administrative burdens.

Through my work with dozens of startups, I've developed a systematic approach to leveraging AI in human resources—what I call the TEAM framework:

T - Talent Acquisition: AI tools that streamline recruiting and help identify promising candidates. This includes resume scanning, preliminary screening chatbots, and AI-assisted interview question generation.

E - Engagement Optimization: AI systems that monitor and enhance team morale and connection. Think sentiment analysis of employee feedback, AI-suggested team-building activities, and personalized recognition programs.

A - Administrative Automation: AI solutions that handle the paperwork and processes that drain human time. This encompasses onboarding document processing, benefits management, and compliance monitoring.

M - Mentorship Amplification: AI that extends the reach of your best leaders by capturing and distributing their wisdom. Knowledge bases with natural language interfaces, AI-facilitated skill development, and performance coaching tools.

The beauty of this framework is that it ensures you're not just randomly applying AI to HR functions, but strategically enhancing the entire people experience, from first contact to ongoing growth.

The essence of team building remains fundamentally human—**empathy, culture, leadership**—and no AI can substitute for these qualities. However, **AI tools can streamline the mechanical aspects of HR and team management**, freeing you to focus on inspiring and leading your team. In other words, let the algorithms handle the tedium so the humans can concentrate on the human elements.

"The most enlightened founders understand that AI in HR isn't about replacing the human in Human Resources—it's about enhancing the human experience at work. When machines handle what machines do best, humans are free to do what only humans can: inspire, empathize, and transform."

AI in Recruiting and Hiring

Finding the right talent is crucial yet challenging. AI can't determine who will fit your culture perfectly, but it can **make your hiring process vastly more efficient**. AI resume screening tools can rapidly scan hundreds of applications and highlight those matching your specific criteria, saving countless hours of manual review.

You can instruct such an AI, *"Identify candidates with at least 3 years of experience in full-stack development and demonstrated expertise in React Native,"* and it will surface the most relevant candidates. Some startups employ AI chatbots to conduct preliminary candidate screenings, asking basic qualification questions before a human interview.

This doesn't replace the interview; it **augments it**—by the time you meet with a candidate (in person or virtually), you already have deeper insight and can use your time to assess the intangible qualities that AI can't measure. **ChatGPT** can even help craft insightful interview questions tailored to specific roles.

If you're hiring your first sales director, you might ask ChatGPT, *"What are 7 behavioral interview questions for a SaaS sales leader that will reveal their approach to building customer relationships?"* This arms you with a structured assessment framework so you feel confident evaluating prospective team members.

Onboarding and Training

Once you begin hiring, effectively onboarding new team members becomes vital. AI tools can streamline this process by automating orientation tasks. For example, you might create a **Notion AI** workspace that new hires can interact with directly: they could ask *"What's our tech stack?"* or *"Who handles payroll questions?"*, and receive immediate answers from your company knowledge base.

This allows newcomers to get answers instantly without requiring constant guidance through every detail. AI can also generate training materials. If you need to train your team on a new software platform your company has adopted, AI like **ChatGPT** can help draft a quick-start guide or even create assessment questions to reinforce learning.

By making training more self-directed with AI assistance, you empower your team to onboard efficiently.

Team Communication and Productivity

A well-coordinated team is a high-performing team. AI can help maintain alignment and communication. One particularly valuable tool many startups embrace is **Fireflies.ai**, an AI meeting assistant. Fireflies can automatically join your Zoom or Teams meetings, **record**

and transcribe the conversation, and then generate a concise summary of discussion points and action items.

Imagine the benefits: no more debating what was decided in last week's meeting or frantically taking notes instead of fully participating. If a team member is unavailable or in a different time zone, they can review the AI-generated meeting summary and quickly catch up. **Key decisions and action items** are highlighted, ensuring nothing falls through the cracks.

This promotes transparency and accountability—everyone knows what's happening, and follow-up responsibilities are crystal clear. As a founder, it also means **you reclaim valuable hours** of your time. As the saying goes, *"Either you run the day or the day runs you."* With AI handling meeting documentation, *you* maintain control of your priorities.

Project management tools are increasingly AI-enhanced. **ClickUp**, a popular project management platform, now features **ClickUp AI** to help draft updates or automate task management. If you need to update a project status, ClickUp's AI can synthesize progress information from task notes. When your team logs daily stand-up updates, the AI might compile a weekly summary of achievements and obstacles.

This means managers spend less time writing reports and more time solving problems. Even scheduling—notoriously time-consuming—becomes easier with AI. Tools like **Clockwise** use AI to optimize calendars, finding optimal meeting times that minimize conflicts and maximize focused work time.

If you've experienced the frustration of email ping-pong trying to coordinate meetings, AI scheduling assistants can manage the back-and-forth of finding common availability, functioning like a human assistant coordinating via email.

Culture and Team Engagement

Here's a surprising area where AI can help: maintaining team engagement and satisfaction. While culture is built through genuine human connection, you can use AI to **regularly assess team morale**. AI-powered survey tools analyze employee feedback sentiment to identify potential issues early.

For example, you might run a monthly anonymous pulse check with questions like *"How supported do you feel by leadership this week?"* or *"Rate your current stress level,"* and the AI will highlight concerning patterns by detecting emotional cues in responses. If something's amiss—perhaps multiple team members feeling overwhelmed by workload—you'll receive early warning to address it proactively.

Some startups also use AI to generate team-building activities or icebreaker questions for meetings (e.g., **"ChatGPT, suggest a creative check-in question for our Friday team call to energize the group"**). It might recommend something engaging like, *"If you could incorporate any AI superpower into our product, what would it be and why?"* which can spark lively discussion and strengthen personal connections.

"The best leaders use AI not to replace human connection but to create more space for it. When algorithms handle the mundane, humans can focus on the meaningful—the conversations, collaborations, and celebrations that truly build teams."

"Take care of your team and they'll take care of your business." AI helps you nurture your team by managing routine HR processes, ensuring clear communication, and even monitoring team wellbeing. But never neglect the personal touch. Use the time AI liberates to **genuinely connect** with your people, recognize their contributions, and build authentic trust. AI can schedule a one-on-one meeting, but the heart-to-heart conversation within that meeting is entirely yours.

In summary, **HR and team building with AI** comes down to this: **employ AI to eliminate barriers**—administrative work, scheduling conflicts, basic information requests—so nothing interferes with creating a great team dynamic. When freed from drowning in operational details, you can truly be the *leader* your team deserves. Your role shifts from taskmaster to **visionary coach**, rallying your team toward a common mission, just as leaders like **Zig Ziglar** and **Jim Rohn** would advocate. AI will handle the background processes; *you* step onto the field and lead your team to victory.

The Resonance Pyramid: AI-Powered Marketing That Connects

Now it's time to **tell the world** about your creation. Marketing and branding can determine a startup's trajectory—you might have the most brilliant solution available, but it means little if nobody knows about it or understands its value. Traditionally, startups with larger budgets dominate marketing channels. But AI has changed that equation, giving resourceful founders **the creative and analytical capabilities of an entire marketing department** at a fraction of the cost.

After years of helping startups leverage AI for growth, I've developed what I call the "Resonance Pyramid"—a hierarchical approach to using AI in marketing that builds from functional to emotional connection:

Level 1: Functional Messaging (Base of Pyramid) At this foundation level, AI helps you clearly articulate what your product or service does. Use AI to generate clear, concise product descriptions, feature lists, and technical explanations. AI excels at transforming complex capabilities into accessible language.

Level 2: Comparative Advantage (Middle Layer) Here, AI helps differentiate your offering from alternatives. Prompt AI to create content that highlights your unique selling propositions, competitive advantages, and key differentiators. This is where data-driven marketing thrives.

Level 3: Emotional Resonance (Pyramid Peak) At the highest level, AI helps craft narratives that forge emotional connections with your audience. While you guide the core story, AI can help you test different emotional angles, personalize messages for specific segments, and find language that triggers deeper engagement.

The key insight: most founders mistakenly start and stop at Level 1, but true marketing magic happens when you build the complete pyramid, using AI as your construction partner at each level.

This is where your venture can *punch significantly above its weight*. As **Steve Jobs** might frame it, if AI is a bicycle for the mind in product creation, in marketing it becomes a **megaphone for your message**. It amplifies your voice, creativity, and reach far beyond what you could achieve alone.

"The greatest marketing illusion is believing humans buy with logic when they actually buy with emotion justified by logic. The most powerful AI marketing doesn't just generate content—it generates emotional resonance, building bridges between your solution and your customer's deepest needs."

Content Creation at Scale

Content is the foundation of modern marketing—whether blog posts, social media updates, newsletters, or video scripts. But producing quality content consistently is resource-intensive. **Enter AI content tools like Jasper and Copy.ai.** These platforms have trained on vast content libraries and can generate remarkably effective copy on nearly any subject.

Imagine you want to create a blog post about the problem your startup solves. You can prompt Jasper, *"Draft a blog post about how AI is transforming small business financial management for non-accountants,"* and it will produce a well-structured draft in seconds. You can then edit it to incorporate your unique insights and voice (AI provides the *framework*, you add the *authenticity* and *expertise*).

Founders use these tools to generate **marketing copy, product descriptions, press releases, and compelling advertising headlines** without requiring a full-time content team from day one. One marketing agency reported saving dozens of hours weekly by using AI to create initial content drafts, enabling their human creatives to focus on refinement and personalization rather than starting from scratch.

For your venture, this means maintaining an active blog or social media presence even with limited resources—the AI becomes your prolific writing partner.

Social Media and Brand Presence

Maintaining consistent engagement across Twitter, LinkedIn, Instagram, and other platforms can feel overwhelming. AI tools simplify this by helping repurpose content and suggesting optimal posting strategies. For example, **ChatGPT** can transform a long-form article you've written into a series of engaging LinkedIn posts or tweets.

You might request, *"Convert this article into 5 standalone Twitter threads with compelling hooks,"* and instantly have a week's worth of social content. Tools like **Buffer** and **Hootsuite** increasingly incorporate AI to recommend the best posting times for maximum engagement, or even to craft post content based on trending topics.

AI can analyze which messaging and visuals perform best with your audience and help you refine your brand voice accordingly. One founder described this advantage: "It's like having a marketing team that never sleeps, constantly analyzing what works and adjusting our approach accordingly."

Branding extends beyond text. **Visual elements matter**, and AI can create these too. Need attention-grabbing graphics but lack a designer? AI image generators can develop illustrations or backgrounds based on simple descriptions. Let's say you need a header image for a blog post about "entrepreneurial resilience."

You could prompt an AI art tool for something like *"a minimalist illustration of a seedling growing through concrete, using our brand color palette"* and iterate until you have a compelling visual that perfectly complements your message. For social media, tools like **Canva** now integrate AI that can generate custom elements or suggest designs—so even without design expertise, you can produce professional-looking content.

Video and Multimedia

Video content drives exceptional engagement but traditionally requires significant production resources—another area where AI provides breakthrough capabilities. We mentioned **Lumen5** earlier: it can transform a blog post or text into a short promotional video automatically, complete with stock footage, animations, and captions.

You simply highlight key messages (or let the AI identify them), select a style template, and Lumen5 generates a polished video that appears professionally produced. **Runway** and similar AI video tools go further: you can generate or edit videos using natural language commands. For instance, *"Replace the background with a modern office scene"* or *"slow down this section by 50%"* can be accomplished without specialized editing skills.

This means you can create advertisements, product demonstrations, or social media clips entirely in-house. And consider **Eleven-Labs**—an AI tool for voice generation. If you need a voiceover for your product demo but can't afford professional voice talent, ElevenLabs can generate realistic human-like narration from your script.

You could have a professional-sounding narration reading content that another AI helped you write, all produced internally. The result? High-quality promotional media created end-to-end by *you and your AI collaborators*, ready to share with your audience.

Marketing Analytics and Strategy

Marketing isn't just about content creation; it's about reaching the right audience and measuring effectiveness. AI plays a crucial role in analytics too. Many marketing platforms now feature AI analytics that automatically segment your audience or highlight significant trends.

For instance, an AI might analyze your website traffic patterns and report, *"Visitors from LinkedIn spend 62% more time on your product pages and have a conversion rate 2.3x higher than traffic from other sources,"* suggesting you should prioritize LinkedIn in your marketing strategy.

AI can also enhance **SEO (Search Engine Optimization)**—tools like **Moz** or **Ahrefs** use AI to recommend keywords to target, content topics trending in your niche, and optimizations for your website to improve search rankings. By implementing AI-generated SEO recommendations (which you can also request from ChatGPT, e.g., *"What are high-value keywords related to sustainable packaging solutions?"*), you strengthen your inbound marketing without requiring specialized SEO expertise.

Consider how powerful this transformation is: previously, you might have needed to hire an SEO consultant, a content writer, a graphic designer, and a social media manager—**now AI can help you perform much of this work independently**, especially during early stages when budgets are constrained. **This doesn't mean you'll never involve specialists as you grow**—but it means you can gain traction and project professionalism immediately, competing effectively against better-funded rivals.

Real-world impact? There are e-commerce founders who, with AI assistance, created hundreds of product descriptions and social media posts in a single weekend—tasks that would have required weeks traditionally—and saw their online traffic double because they maintained fresh, keyword-optimized content publishing. Another founder expanded to international markets by using AI translation tools: they created content in English and used AI to translate and culturally adapt it for Spanish and French markets, dramatically extending their reach without hiring multiple translators.

"Marketing communicates value. AI doesn't change what you communicate—your authentic story and unique value to customers—but it supercharges how you communicate. It ensures your message reaches more people, in more channels, in more compelling ways."

A word of wisdom: maintain your **brand authenticity**. AI can generate abundant content, but quantity should never supersede quality and authenticity. Use AI output as a starting point or collaborative tool, but infuse your brand's distinct personality. Review and refine what it produces; ensure it sounds genuinely like *you*. The most successful AI-powered marketers treat the technology as a creative assistant, not an autopilot. You provide the strategic direction ("this is our brand voice, these are our values"), and let AI handle the execution.

Finally, marketing requires continuous experimentation. Use AI's analytical feedback to refine your strategy: amplify what works, pivot away from what doesn't. In this sense, AI functions as a trusted advisor consistently providing insights to inform your marketing decisions. And when it comes to branding, consistency is essential—AI helps ensure every tweet, blog post, video, and email aligns with the story you want to tell. With AI by your side, your small marketing team (or solo effort) transforms into a **comprehensive multi-channel campaign** that builds a loyal community around your startup.

The Visibility Vault: Using AI to Master Financial Intelligence

Every founder recognizes that **cash flow and operations** form the lifeblood of a startup. While not as glamorous as innovation or as exciting as product launches, *operational excellence and financial discipline* often determine whether your venture thrives or falters. Here too, AI proves invaluable—it's like having a tireless analyst and operations manager overseeing the details, preventing you from becoming overwhelmed by administrative minutiae.

One of the most transformative applications of AI for founders is what I call building a "Visibility Vault"—a comprehensive financial intelligence system that gives you unprecedented clarity into your business:

Chamber 1: Historical Analysis AI tools that process your past financial data to identify patterns invisible to the human eye. Not just what happened, but why it happened and what it means.

Chamber 2: Present Monitoring AI systems that track current financial health in real-time, flagging anomalies before they become problems and highlighting opportunities before they disappear.

Chamber 3: Future Modeling AI forecasting that presents not just one future but multiple potential scenarios based on different variables, letting you explore "what if" questions with sophisticated sensitivity analysis.

Chamber 4: Decision Augmentation AI advisors that don't just present data but offer suggested actions based on your stated goals, risk tolerance, and previous decisions.

The founders who build a complete Visibility Vault gain an almost unfair advantage—they operate with a level of financial intelligence that makes competitors look like they're flying blind. More importantly, they shift from reactive to proactive financial management.

The objective is straightforward: **use AI to work smarter behind the scenes**, so your company operates with clockwork precision while you avoid costly missteps. Consider all those routine reports and repetitive tasks that consume hours of attention—what if most of that could be handled or at least prepared by an AI assistant, allowing you to concentrate on strategic decisions? This is where AI in operations and finance becomes transformative for founders, especially those without a dedicated CFO or COO in the early stages.

"The difference between a founder who survives and one who thrives often comes down to financial visibility. AI doesn't just count your money faster—it transforms your relationship with numbers from record-keeping to strategic intelligence. When your financial data becomes a crystal ball rather than a rearview mirror, your decision-making enters a new dimension."

Bookkeeping and Financial Management

Let's begin with managing the money. **QuickBooks**, the widely-used accounting software, now features an AI-powered assistant called **Intuit Assist**. This isn't traditional bookkeeping; Intuit Assist can *automate numerous accounting functions*. For instance, it can translate natural language into accounting actions.

If you forward your AI assistant an email from a vendor stating *"Attached is the invoice for last month's consulting services, $2,500 due in 21 days,"* Intuit Assist can automatically generate that as a new bill in QuickBooks. It can process a photo of a receipt or a PDF invoice and create a proper expense entry. It also provides intelligent reminders: it will **detect overdue invoices and prompt you (or even automatically send a professional reminder to the client)** to ensure timely payment.

Essentially, the AI tracks accounts receivable and payable, ensuring nothing slips through the cracks. One of its most valuable capabilities is **expense categorization**—a tedious task when done manually. Intuit Assist learns from your previous inputs (recognizing, for example, that charges from "Adobe Creative Suite" should always be categorized under Software Expenses) and begins performing this categorization automatically, dramatically reducing time spent on monthly reconciliations.

Dave Talach, a QuickBooks executive, captured the benefit perfectly when he explained the goal is to *"eliminate that minutiae... so [business owners] can focus on speaking with customers."* Less time on accounting tedium means more time for strategy, sales, and product development—the activities that *grow* your business.

Beyond QuickBooks, tools like **Fyle** or **Expensify** use AI to automatically scan receipts and prepare expense reports. If you've ever spent a weekend sorting through accumulated receipts (or procrastinated until tax season), you understand how transformative this capability is. By connecting your financial accounts and credit cards, AI systems can monitor your transactions and immediately flag unusual activity or prepare regular cash flow summaries.

Imagine receiving a Monday morning report in your inbox, automatically generated: *"You spent $1,200 on software subscriptions last quarter, a 40% increase over previous quarters. Three subscriptions appear to have overlapping functionality. Review recommended consolidation options below."* That's AI functioning as your financial guardian.

"The best financial decisions aren't made in the rear-view mirror of last quarter's statements, but in the real-time dashboard of today's transactions. AI transforms financial management from historical record-keeping to proactive strategy."

Financial Planning and Analysis

AI isn't limited to recording history; it excels at forecasting the future. Founders can leverage AI for financial modeling and scenario analysis. AI-driven financial planning tools can project your cash runway based on various assumptions. You might ask, *"How would our runway change if customer acquisition costs increase by 30% but retention improves by 15%?"* and receive instant scenario comparisons.

Tools like **Pigment** and emerging fintech AI platforms provide conversational interfaces to financial data. Even without spreadsheet expertise, you can query your data in natural language and receive insights. **ChatGPT** itself, when given appropriate data, can analyze and identify patterns. For example, paste in a simplified income statement and ask, *"Where do you see opportunities to improve margins?"*—it might observe that your cloud infrastructure costs are disproportionately high compared to industry benchmarks or suggest negotiating better terms with key suppliers.

In fact, AI can analyze your financial data and identify cost-cutting opportunities or spending optimizations. While you'd need to provide this data carefully to maintain privacy, this can be done with anonymized information or percentages. The key benefit: AI can function as a financial advisor, highlighting inefficiencies and opportunities that might otherwise go unnoticed.

Operations and Process Efficiency

Operations encompasses a broad spectrum—from supply chain to customer service to internal processes. Let's explore several areas where AI creates operational advantages:

Customer Service & Support

In early stages, you might lack dedicated support staff, meaning you personally handle customer inquiries. AI can significantly lighten this burden. Deploying a **chatbot** on your website or app can address common questions instantly. Services like **Intercom** now offer AI chatbots that can utilize your knowledge base to answer customer questions autonomously.

For instance, if a customer asks, *"How do I reset my account password?"*—the AI bot can immediately provide step-by-step instructions. If a question becomes too complex or the bot lacks sufficient information, it can seamlessly transfer to you or a team member. The outcome? Customers receive prompt responses around the clock, and you only intervene when truly necessary, rather than repeatedly answering the same basic questions.

Exceptional customer service translates to higher satisfaction and retention, achieved with minimal additional effort through AI assistance.

Scheduling and Logistics

Operational management frequently involves scheduling—whether production runs, delivery routes, or simply coordinating meetings. **AI scheduling tools** can optimize various timetables. If your startup includes a delivery component, AI routing software can determine the most efficient paths for drivers, reducing fuel costs and time (similar to what logistics giants like UPS employ, now accessible to small businesses).

If your business manages inventory, AI can forecast demand patterns so you maintain optimal stock levels—not excessive (tying up capital) and not insufficient (missing sales opportunities). These predictive algorithms were once enterprise-only capabilities; now many are available to small businesses through accessible software platforms.

Knowledge Management and Documentation

We highlighted **Fireflies.ai** for meeting transcription earlier, but from an operational perspective, having a searchable archive of all meeting discussions provides tremendous value. It becomes part of your institutional knowledge. Months later, if you vaguely recall discussing a particular marketing initiative, you could search your AI-generated meeting records for "Instagram campaign strategy" and instantly locate when it was discussed and what was decided.

This represents operational knowledge at your fingertips. **Notion AI** similarly helps by summarizing lengthy documents or Slack conversations, enabling you to extract key information without sifting through excessive detail.

Task Automation

Many operational tasks are ideal candidates for automation. If you regularly perform repetitive activities—perhaps sorting incoming emails or transferring data between systems—there's likely an AI solution available. **Zapier**, while not AI-specific, connects different applications and can incorporate AI in triggers (such as "if an email contains these keywords or sentiment, perform this action").

Modern AI tools can even observe how you complete digital tasks and then replicate them. Startups increasingly use robotic process automation (RPA) with AI for functions like generating weekly metrics reports: the RPA bot collects data from various sources, the AI synthesizes insights ("customer retention improved 12% this month, primarily in the enterprise segment"), and you receive the complete analysis without manual effort.

Staying Organized and Informed

Operational excellence requires meticulous organization. **ClickUp** (with its AI capabilities) or **Asana** help ensure projects remain on track, as previously mentioned. But consider AI for **document management** as well. Need to locate a specific contractual clause among dozens of legal documents? AI search tools can find that needle in the haystack instantly.

Need to draft a contract or policy? ChatGPT can produce a solid initial version of a standard NDA or service agreement, which you can then have an attorney review—saving billable hours by completing the foundational work in advance.

A particularly powerful operational application of AI is **risk monitoring**. For example, an AI could monitor industry news or regulatory updates and alert you to developments that might impact your business (such as new privacy legislation affecting technology companies). This type of intelligent monitoring functions as an early warning system—something small companies traditionally couldn't afford.

These improvements in finances and operations deliver one crucial benefit: **peace of mind**. Instead of constantly firefighting or worrying that something important was overlooked, you have AI assistants standing vigilant. Your finances receive tighter oversight (without requiring your constant attention), and your operations become streamlined and efficient. It's comparable to having a full-time analyst, accountant, and operations manager, except they work tirelessly and economically.

The renowned management thinker **Peter Drucker** taught that *"what gets measured gets managed."* AI helps you **measure and monitor everything that matters** in your business. It's like having a comprehensive dashboard where every important metric is continuously tracked. Leverage this capability. The confidence gained from knowing your numbers and processes are under control will empower you to take bold action in growing your venture. **You can drive faster because you trust the instrumentation in your cockpit.**

Running a startup inevitably brings stress—that's inherent to the journey—but with AI handling finances and operations, you eliminate a substantial portion of avoidable anxiety. You won't lie awake worrying about forgotten invoices or uncertain cash projections; the AI will have reminded you, or forecast for you, well in advance. **This is**

how you accelerate with intelligence: not just moving faster, but also smarter and more securely. Your startup becomes not merely agile, but resilient.

The Founder's AI Ethical Framework

As we harness AI's power, we must also acknowledge our responsibility as stewards of this technology. Through my journey and conversations with thoughtful entrepreneurs, I've developed what I call the "Three Horizons of AI Ethics" that every founder should consider:

Horizon 1: Company Integrity At this first level, we ask: How do we use AI responsibly within our own operations? This includes considerations like data privacy, bias monitoring, transparency with customers about AI usage, and ensuring human oversight where appropriate.

Horizon 2: Stakeholder Impact At the second level, we consider: How does our AI implementation affect everyone connected to our business? This encompasses impacts on employees (job transformation, not elimination), customers (enhanced rather than manipulated experiences), and partners (fair value creation).

Horizon 3: Societal Contribution At the furthest horizon, we contemplate: How does our use of AI shape the world we want to build? Here we consider whether our AI applications advance beneficial innovation, promote inclusion, and align with sustainable development.

I've found that founders who deliberately address all three horizons not only avoid potential pitfalls but actually gain competitive advantages: deeper customer trust, stronger team alignment, and more resilient business models prepared for evolving regulations.

The most successful entrepreneurs don't view ethics as a constraint on innovation but as a compass that guides it toward more meaningful and sustainable outcomes.

"The founders who will define the next decade aren't just asking 'Can we build this with AI?' but 'Should we build this with AI?' And when they find the intersection of could and should—where technological possibility meets ethical imperative—that's where the truly transformative companies are born."

Wisdom From the Frontlines: Lessons From Founders Using AI

Nothing resonates more powerfully than authentic stories of entrepreneurs who have walked this path and achieved success. Let's examine **founders who have embraced AI** in their journey, and the practical lessons we can learn from their experiences. These aren't distant hypotheticals—they're individuals like you who decided to accelerate their startup growth by partnering with AI tools.

Their stories highlight the day-to-day impact of AI and carry a unifying message: *founders who harness AI effectively can achieve results far beyond their apparent resources.*

Lesson 1: AI Can Bridge Skill Gaps and Enable Solo Success

We previously discussed **Josh Mohrer of Wave** in the product development section, but his story deserves deeper examination for the lessons it offers. Josh had a vision for an AI-driven app (transcribing and summarizing audio notes) but lacked formal engineering training. Traditionally, a non-technical founder might be forced to recruit a technical co-founder or invest heavily in development talent.

Instead, Josh turned to ChatGPT as his coding mentor and collaborator. *"ChatGPT got me kind of the rest of the way there,"* he explained about building the first version of his application. This represents a profound shift. The lesson: **Don't be deterred if you lack specific expertise—AI can help fill critical knowledge gaps.** Josh's Wave app, now serving thousands of users, stands as compelling evidence.

He discovered that with patience and determination, AI tools can not only assist but also *teach* as you build. Whenever he encountered a coding challenge, he would ask ChatGPT to explain the concept or troubleshoot the code. It functioned like an expert consultant available at any moment. For aspiring founders, the takeaway is transformative: AI lowers entry barriers dramatically; lacking certain skills is no longer an insurmountable obstacle but rather a challenge you can navigate with AI guidance.

"The most successful entrepreneurs aren't necessarily those who know everything—they're those who know how to find what they need when they need it. AI makes that search instantaneous, turning knowledge gaps into stepping stones rather than barriers."

Lesson 2: Speed and Efficiency Become Your Competitive Edge With AI

Consider the experience of *Elena*, who launched an e-commerce startup selling sustainable home goods. As the only employee initially, she faced overwhelming marketing demands. Elena leveraged **Jasper** to create engaging product descriptions and advertising copy, and **Canva's AI tools** to design professional product images.

What would have consumed a week of effort (or required budget for a marketer and designer) she accomplished in a single day. The outcome? She could launch campaigns faster than competitors with larger teams. When seasonal opportunities emerged, she had fresh content ready the next morning while larger rivals were still holding planning meetings.

Her agility translated into an engaged social media following and impressive early sales growth. Elena's lesson: **AI provides extraordinary leverage.** It allowed her to *accomplish the work of many* in a fraction of the time. Her advice to fellow founders is to identify the tasks consuming the most time and determine if an AI solution exists to streamline them.

In her case, content creation and design were the major time demands, and AI transformed these into quick, almost effortless activities. This enabled her to redirect her attention to negotiating better supplier terms and enhancing customer experience—elements that further differentiated her brand in a competitive market.

Lesson 3: AI Liberates Founders to Focus on High-Value Human Connections

A fintech startup founder, *Raj*, integrated AI throughout his operations (implementing QuickBooks' Intuit Assist, automating customer support with a chatbot, and scheduling social content with AI tools). He discovered that after establishing these systems, he spent 30% less time weekly on routine administrative tasks.

How did he invest this reclaimed time? He personally called five customers every week to express appreciation and gather feedback. This human touch yielded profound customer insights and product improvement ideas, and those customers became enthusiastic advocates for his platform (the personal connection with the founder created lasting loyalty).

Raj attributes this to AI: "Without the hours freed by automation, I simply wouldn't have had the bandwidth to build these relationships." His startup's user retention and referral rates increased significantly because of these efforts. The lesson here: **use the "gift of time" AI provides wisely**. Invest it in activities that truly impact outcomes—often the human connections or strategic thinking that only you can provide.

As **Jim Rohn** would emphasize, *spend your time where it creates the greatest value*. Automation isn't about doing less work; it's about doing **more meaningful work**. Raj noted, "The irony is that AI made my business more human, not less—because it handled the mechanical so I could focus on the personal."

Lesson 4: Stay Curious and Continuously Experiment With New AI Capabilities

Founders who derive maximum benefit from AI maintain a learning mindset. An exemplar is **Dave Rogenmoser, co-founder of Jasper AI**—while he's building an AI company, his journey to explosive growth with Jasper was propelled by continuously exploring new ways to reach customers using AI marketing. He famously scaled Jasper from zero to substantial revenue by leveraging AI for content creation and relentless marketing experimentation.

Similarly, other successful founders monitor AI developments closely: when **GPT-4** was released, they immediately asked, *"How can this new capability enhance our workflow or product?"* Some integrated AI directly into their offerings, providing AI-powered features to users before competitors could respond.

The universal lesson: **the AI landscape evolves rapidly; entrepreneurs who learn and adapt will ride the wave, while those who hesitate risk being left behind.** Don't postpone exploring AI tools. Schedule regular time to experiment with new capabilities, attend industry webinars on AI applications, or connect with other founders about their AI implementation strategies.

Each advancement (whether improved text-to-image generation or AI agents capable of performing complex multi-step tasks) could unlock efficiency gains or even pivot opportunities for your business.

Lesson 5: Mindset Matters—View AI as a Team Member, Not Just a Tool

This lesson is more philosophical but evident across successful case studies. The most effective founders discuss AI as an extension of their team. They "delegate" responsibilities to it, trust it with appropriate tasks (while verifying outcomes), and "collaborate" with it by providing clear instructions and feedback.

Founders who struggled often expected immediate perfection or treated AI as an inscrutable black box they didn't want to understand. The lesson is to cultivate a collaborative mindset: **you + AI = team**. For example, if AI-generated marketing content doesn't align with your brand voice initially, instead of concluding "this doesn't work," successful founders think, "how can I guide it to improve? Perhaps I need to provide better examples or refine my prompts."

This mirrors how you'd coach a team member rather than dismissing a tool as broken. The result is a virtuous cycle: the more you work with AI, the better *you* become at leveraging it (developing prompt engineering skills, understanding its strengths and limitations), and the better results it delivers.

"The founders who extract the most value from AI are those who approach it not as users of a tool but as conductors of an orchestra—providing direction, refining the performance, and knowing when each instrument should take the lead or fall silent."

To summarize these lessons: **AI empowers founders of all backgrounds to achieve more with greater speed.** It levels the competitive landscape, enabling a small startup to operate with the capabilities of a much larger organization. But the winners treat AI as an enabler, not a replacement for initiative. They remain focused on delivering value, using AI to amplify their efforts, not substitute for their vision.

They also navigate limitations ethically—recognizing AI can sometimes produce inaccurate or biased output, so they maintain human oversight for critical communications (especially public or sensitive content).

These real-world founder stories emphasize one overarching principle—*AI rewards the doers.* As **Zig Ziglar** might express it, *"Go as far as you can see; when you get there, you'll be able to see farther."* Begin with a single AI tool, apply it purposefully, and your horizon will expand to reveal more possibilities. Each positive result builds confidence to explore the next application. Before long, you'll have integrated AI throughout your startup's operations and strategy, wondering how you ever managed without it.

Your AI Acceleration Roadmap: Final Thoughts and Call to Action

As you stand at this intersection of entrepreneurship and artificial intelligence, remember that technology alone doesn't create success—vision does. AI is the wind at your back, but you determine the destination. The founders who thrive in this new landscape won't be those with the most advanced algorithms, but those who most artfully combine human wisdom with computational power.

Your advantage isn't just having access to AI—it's having the courage to reimagine your entire business through the lens of augmented intelligence. While others ask "Can AI help with this specific task?" you should be asking "How would my entire industry transform if intelligence were unlimited?"

This is your moment. The tools described in this chapter aren't futuristic possibilities—they're available now, waiting for you to harness them. The only question is whether you'll be among the pioneers who leverage them to create new value or among those who watch from the sidelines as their competitive landscape transforms without them.

Start small if you must, but start today. Identify one area where AI could amplify your impact, and take that first step. Remember, the distance between ordinary companies and extraordinary ones is often just a matter of courage—the courage to embrace new capabilities and reimagine what's possible.

Knowledge alone won't transform your startup; *applying* it will. The world of AI presents an extraordinary toolkit, but you must actively employ these capabilities. As motivational speaker **Tony Robbins** emphasizes, *"Knowledge is not power. Knowledge is only potential power. Action is power."* The same wisdom echoes through the teachings of **Jim Rohn** and **Zig Ziglar**—it's through doing that dreams materialize. Let's convert motivation into momentum.

Start Now, Start Small

You don't need to implement everything you've learned simultaneously. In fact, that would be counterproductive. The key is to begin *somewhere*. Select one area of your business that causes frustration or consumes disproportionate time. Perhaps you struggle with writing marketing content, or your financial tracking is disorganized, or you have a backlog of ideas you never find time to explore.

Choose one challenge and commit to applying an AI solution to it this week. Register for that tool's free trial, dedicate an evening to experimenting with it. The initial experience might feel slightly awkward—new technologies often do—but recall our discussion about "risking the unusual" to avoid settling for the ordinary. **Courage** bridges the gap between thinking and doing.

Have the boldness to experiment with AI in your startup. The potential gains far outweigh the risks; most of these tools offer free or low-cost trials, and the upside is reclaiming hours of your life while accelerating your business momentum.

Leadership Mindset: Captain an Augmented Team

As you embrace AI, reconceptualize your role. You're not a solo founder overwhelmed by tasks; you're the **commander of a team** that includes both humans and AI assistants. This perspective shift is powerful. When you assign your AI meeting assistant to handle note-taking, you're delegating as an effective leader. When you use ChatGPT to explore potential strategies, you're facilitating a brainstorming session with your AI collaborator.

Exceptional leaders leverage all available resources—and you now have an unprecedented class of resources at your disposal. Adopt the mindset that you *deserve* this leverage. It's not cutting corners; it's working intelligently and modernly. Using AI to handle routine work demonstrates respect for your own time and talents, allowing you to apply yourself where you create maximum impact. **Your creativity + artificial intelligence = an unbeatable combination.**

Remember **Steve Jobs'** famous analogy about computers being bicycles for the mind? Envision AI as a fleet of supercharged vehicles—or perhaps rockets—for the entrepreneurial mind. The distance between vision and reality shrinks dramatically when you harness these accelerators. But *you* still navigate and set the destination. **Your vision, values, and creativity remain the guiding force.** AI will support your direction.

"When an entrepreneur's intuition meets AI's analytical horsepower, the impossible becomes achievable, the complex becomes clear, and the future becomes now."

Continuous Growth: Stay Inspired and Never Stop Learning

The AI landscape evolves at breathtaking speed. Today's cutting-edge capabilities become tomorrow's standard features. This constant evolution creates endless opportunities for the alert and adaptable founder. Make it a habit to nurture your knowledge about innovation. Follow founders who use AI effectively, connect with thought leaders who explain AI breakthroughs in accessible terms, perhaps take a brief online course in prompt engineering or AI business applications.

The more you learn, the more possibilities you'll discover for implementing AI in innovative ways. **Zig Ziglar** observed, *"People often say motivation doesn't last. Well, neither does bathing—that's why we recommend it daily."* Maintain your motivation by envisioning what your startup can become with the right tools and consistent effort. Surround yourself (even virtually) with innovation communities—that mindset is contagious.

As a practical step, create an action list after finishing this chapter: identify 3 AI tools mentioned that you haven't yet explored but could benefit your business. Next to each, note one concrete application (e.g., "Test Fireflies.ai on our next team meeting," or "Use ChatGPT to draft our email newsletter template"). This becomes your implementation roadmap. Post it visibly or save it as your priority task list. **Execution is where transformation happens.** As you complete each item, you'll not only achieve immediate improvements but also develop an "AI-first" approach to business challenges.

Embrace the Journey

Implementing AI in your startup represents an ongoing journey, not a one-time project. You might experiment with a tool that doesn't perfectly address your needs initially—that's perfectly normal. Treat it as a learning experience and adjust your approach. Your first AI-generated content might not capture your brand voice precisely; refine the prompts and it improves. Your first AI-designed graphic might not match your vision; adjust your instructions or try another tool.

This iterative process embodies the startup ethos itself: build, measure, learn, repeat. You're applying the same methodology to AI integration. And with each cycle, you're *accelerating*. Your knowledge compounds. Soon, tasks that consumed days might require only hours, and initiatives that seemed unreachable due to resource constraints become entirely feasible.

"Yesterday's entrepreneurs competed on who could work the hardest. Today's entrepreneurs compete on who can work the smartest. Tomorrow's winners will be those who master the art of human-AI collaboration, creating symphonies of innovation beyond what either could achieve alone."

The future belongs to those who build it. With AI as your ally, what future will you create?

10

—•—

Going Public — The IPO Journey Unveiled

The Ultimate Milestone: Understanding the IPO

Imagine the day your startup steps onto the grandest stage in business. An **Initial Public Offering (IPO)** represents that momentous debut—but it's not merely a financial transaction or regulatory milestone. It's more accurately described as a company's graduation ceremony, wedding day, and Olympic competition all merged into one defining event. This is when your private company offers shares to the public and transforms into a publicly traded entity. In essence, it's when *your company "goes public."* This matters profoundly because it marks a watershed moment: suddenly, anyone (from institutional investors to everyday individuals) can purchase ownership in your company through a stock exchange.

For a founder, an IPO often feels like **validation of years of relentless work**—a moment when the market formally recognizes your company as mature and successful enough to trade on the open market. For investors and the public, an IPO presents an opportunity to participate in a company's next chapter of growth from the ground floor.

"An IPO isn't the finish line—it's the starting gun of a new race, one with more spectators, higher expectations, and greater rewards for those who continue to lead with vision and execution."

From a **founder's perspective**, an IPO typically serves multiple strategic objectives. First, it provides access to significant capital to fuel further expansion or retire earlier debts. It's also the moment when early supporters (including you, your team, and initial investors) can finally *realize the value* they've built: after years of creating equity, they can sell portions of their holdings and reap tangible rewards.

In fact, an IPO is often viewed as an *"exit strategy"* for early investors—a mechanism to convert their paper gains into actual returns after supporting the company's growth journey. From an **investor's perspective**, an IPO matters because it opens access to a high-potential company previously restricted to a select few. It's comparable to attending the premiere of a highly anticipated film—early public investors hope to buy into a promising enterprise and potentially see their investment multiply as the company realizes its full potential.

In essence, an IPO represents a transformative event: your company transitions from the private domain (with a limited number of owners) to the public arena, bringing new opportunities, resources, and responsibilities.

The Decision Point: Why Companies Choose to Go Public

Why would a company take this significant leap into the public spotlight? It's like deciding to perform on Broadway after years of rehearsing in community theater—exhilarating, terrifying, and potentially transformative. Several compelling motivations drive this momentous decision—these are the primary catalysts that propel founders to ring that iconic exchange bell.

Access to Substantial Capital for Growth

The foremost reason is to raise **significant funding** to invest in the business. By selling shares to the public, companies can accumulate a substantial capital influx in a single coordinated event. This capital can finance new product development, market expansion, strategic hiring, or even acquisitions of complementary businesses.

Essentially, an IPO can provide the fuel needed for the next stage of growth that might be challenging to secure through private funding alone. The public markets offer a depth of capital that few private sources can match, making IPOs particularly attractive for companies with ambitious expansion plans.

Liquidity for Founders and Early Investors

Going public creates a mechanism for early stakeholders to convert portions of their ownership into liquid assets. If you've invested years of effort (and perhaps substantial personal resources) into building your venture, an IPO gives you the opportunity to **finally monetize some of that value**. Early investors like venture capitalists or angel investors similarly gain a pathway to realize returns on their initial risk-taking.

In other words, an IPO can serve as a *reward for the vision and commitment* demonstrated by those who believed in the company from its earliest stages. This liquidity event doesn't necessarily mean founders cash out entirely—most continue to hold significant stakes—but it provides financial flexibility previously unavailable.

Enhanced Company Prestige and Brand Recognition

A distinct prestige accompanies public company status. Listing on a major exchange can elevate your company's profile substantially. Suddenly, your organization appears in financial news, analysts regularly discuss its performance, and it gains credibility with customers and partners.

Being public often **increases visibility and strengthens market perception**, which can even boost sales—customers may place greater trust in a brand that has successfully navigated the rigorous scrutiny of the IPO due diligence process. It's comparable to relocating your business to the most prominent address in town; visibility and perceived legitimacy increase dramatically.

"**Going public transforms your company from a private conversation among insiders to a global dialogue with the market. Every achievement becomes more visible, every milestone more celebrated, and every misstep more scrutinized. The spotlight intensifies everything.**"

Using Stock as Strategic Currency

Public stock can function as a powerful form of currency. For example, you can acquire other companies by offering your own company's shares as consideration. It also becomes easier to attract and retain exceptional talent by offering stock options or grants with clear market value (since your equity is publicly traded).

Essentially, going public provides a new strategic tool—your stock—which can be deployed for growth initiatives and incentivizing employees. This "acquisition currency" becomes particularly valuable in consolidating markets or expanding through strategic combinations.

Future Fundraising Flexibility and Stability

Once public, a company can more readily raise additional capital through *secondary offerings* (issuing more stock later) or by leveraging its public status to secure favorable financing terms. Being an established public company generally means **improved access to capital markets** going forward—investors typically have greater comfort funding a known public entity with transparent reporting.

Additionally, the discipline and disclosure required of public companies can instill stronger operational practices and potentially result in better credit terms from lenders. Public companies often enjoy more stability in their access to capital, even during challenging economic periods when private funding might contract.

From a motivational perspective, choosing to go public represents **embracing an expanded vision**. It's declaring, "We believe our company is ready for the world stage, and we welcome the accountability that comes with it." Every founder's specific motivation might differ—some pursue IPOs to accelerate growth, others because market conditions are optimal, and some because it represents the **natural evolution** of their company's journey. Whatever the driver, it's a decision requiring careful consideration, but when aligned with your company's strategic objectives, an IPO can become a powerful catalyst for your next phase of success.

Behind the Curtain: The IPO Process Step by Step

Going public isn't an overnight transformation—it's more accurately described as a marathon with distinct phases. Think of it as preparing for a grand **opening night performance**: you must rehearse extensively, prepare the venue, promote the event, and finally raise the curtain. Here's a detailed roadmap of the IPO journey:

1. Preparation and Building Your Advisory Team

First, a company considering an IPO must ensure its fundamentals are solid. This means confirming your financial records are impeccable, your business model demonstrates sustainability, and any potential issues (legal or operational) have been addressed. Most companies will engage an **investment bank (or consortium of banks)** to act as underwriters—these financial specialists guide you through the IPO process and help market your stock to potential investors.

When selecting investment banks, founders typically evaluate the bank's reputation, industry expertise, and track record with similar IPOs. This decision deserves careful consideration—the investment bank becomes your crucial partner in shaping your IPO strategy and ultimately determining its success.

"Choosing your IPO partners is like selecting your expedition team for climbing Everest—their experience, reputation, and compatibility with your vision can make the difference between reaching the summit triumphantly or turning back halfway."

2. Due Diligence and Regulatory Filing

Once your team is assembled, an intensive period of **due diligence** commences. Imagine opening every drawer and examining every corner of your company—that's the thoroughness this phase demands. The underwriters and your legal counsel will meticulously review financial statements, contracts, customer metrics, intellectual property, and virtually every aspect of your business to ensure everything is properly structured.

You'll prepare a comprehensive document called a **prospectus** (part of the regulatory filing, typically a Form S-1 in the U.S.) that provides potential investors with detailed information about your business: your financial performance, intended use of IPO proceeds, risk factors, competitive landscape, and the company's complete story. This document undergoes rigorous review by regulators (such as the Securities and Exchange Commission in the U.S.) for accuracy and completeness.

It's often initially submitted as a draft (sometimes referred to as a "red herring" prospectus until finalized). Expect multiple rounds of questions and revisions from regulators—you'll be meticulously addressing every detail to meet disclosure requirements. This phase is crucial because it compels the company to *present its complete narrative with unprecedented transparency.*

3. Marketing the IPO (The Roadshow)

With a prospectus in hand (even if preliminary), you and your underwriters embark on what's known as a **roadshow**. This represents the marketing campaign for your IPO. The company's senior leadership (typically the CEO and CFO) present the business to institutional investors—large entities like mutual funds, pension funds, and investment firms likely to purchase significant portions of the offering.

You might travel to financial centers across the country or internationally, delivering presentations, answering detailed questions, and **generating enthusiasm** about your stock. Consider it a *focused sales pitch for your company's future potential.* During this period, the underwriters discreetly gauge market interest and potential pricing. Investors might indicate, "We're impressed with the company and would consider investing at approximately $22 per share." This feedback helps determine the demand for your stock.

4. Pricing and Going Public

As the roadshow concludes, your underwriters consolidate all indications of interest and determine the optimal IPO **price per share**. This represents a critical decision—price too high and the stock might struggle once trading begins; price too low and you leave money on the table. Using the collected feedback (the orders investors have submitted) and considering current market conditions, the bank recommends a price (typically within a previously advertised range).

The evening before the big day, you finalize the price and number of shares to be offered. Once you and the bankers reach agreement and regulators provide final clearance, the IPO mechanism activates. On the morning of the IPO, shares are officially **released to the public**

market—your company now appears on a major exchange (like the NYSE or NASDAQ) and trading commences!

This often includes a ceremonial bell-ringing at the exchange or other celebratory event. It's an emotionally charged and exhilarating moment—within minutes, you'll watch your stock price respond as public investors begin trading shares.

5. Aftermarket Stabilization and Life as a Public Company

In the immediate aftermath of the IPO, the underwriters may continue supporting the stock's stability if necessary (for example, they might purchase shares if the price drops too significantly, using a mechanism known as a "greenshoe" option). But very quickly, your stock price becomes entirely subject to market forces. Your company now has **hundreds or thousands of shareholders**, and you must conduct quarterly earnings calls, file regular regulatory reports, and meet corporate governance requirements.

This transition requires adapting to public company standards with heightened scrutiny and transparency. You'll likely expand your board of directors if you haven't already, and decision-making processes may become more formalized compared to your startup phase. It's comparable to a graduation—the celebration concludes, and then the real work continues on a larger stage. The positive news is you've secured the capital and recognition you sought; the challenge is consistently performing and **communicating transparently** to maintain your new shareholders' confidence.

Throughout this process, **founders should rely on experienced advisors**—skilled lawyers, investment bankers, and mentors who have navigated IPOs previously. The journey can be intense, but understanding these stages demystifies it. Rather than viewing it as a leap into the unknown, you can approach it as a series of manageable tasks. Each step, from preparation to pricing, becomes achievable with the right team and mindset. By breaking it down into these components, the concept of taking your company public becomes less intimidating and more of a structured project you can methodically plan and execute.

Weighing the Balance: Pros and Cons of Going Public

Before committing to this journey, it's essential to carefully evaluate the **advantages and disadvantages** of an IPO. Going public presents a double-edged sword—it offers remarkable opportunities but also introduces new challenges. Let's examine the key considerations from both perspectives:

The Upside: Why Going Public Can Be Transformative

Significant Capital Raised

As discussed, an IPO can **infuse your company with substantial capital**. These funds can accelerate growth initiatives—entering new markets, developing products more rapidly, or strengthening your operational infrastructure. Unlike loans, IPO proceeds don't require repayment; they represent investment in exchange for equity in your business.

Liquidity and Wealth Creation

By going public, you establish a market for your shares. Founders, employees, and early investors holding equity finally gain a mechanism to convert portions of their holdings into liquid assets (subject to lock-up periods and trading windows). This can be life-changing on a personal level—years of dedication transforming into tangible wealth—and it **rewards the team** that believed in the company from the beginning.

Enhanced Credibility and Market Visibility

A public listing typically confers a halo of credibility. Your company appears in financial news, market indices, and analyst reports. This elevated profile can help secure **better partnerships and commer-**

cial opportunities. For example, potential business partners may feel increased confidence working with a company that has successfully completed the rigorous IPO process and maintains transparent financial reporting.

This enhanced credibility also aids recruitment efforts: top talent may feel greater security joining a public company, and you can attract them with equity compensation that has clear, publicly established value. The market recognition that comes with public status can become a powerful competitive advantage in multiple dimensions of your business.

Easier Access to Future Capital

Once public, if your company performs well, you generally enjoy *more favorable and efficient access to additional funding*. You could issue additional shares through secondary offerings to raise capital relatively quickly. Additionally, financial institutions might offer more attractive lending terms because of your established equity base and regular disclosure practices.

Being public can substantially lower your **cost of capital**, meaning fundraising or borrowing may become less expensive than it would be as a private entity. This financial flexibility represents a significant strategic advantage as you pursue continued growth.

Stock as Acquisition Currency and Employee Incentive

Public stock becomes a powerful tool for strategic growth. You can propose acquisitions where you pay partially or entirely with your own shares, which target companies may find attractive since the stock is easily valued and traded. It also simplifies implementing employee ownership programs; team members can track their equity value in real-time and participate directly in the company's success, potentially increasing motivation and retention.

This ability to use stock as currency enhances your strategic flexibility in both external growth initiatives and internal talent management.

"Public company stock is like having a universal currency in the business world—suddenly you can make acquisitions, attract talent, and raise capital with a liquidity and efficiency that private companies can only dream of."

The Challenges: What to Watch For

Loss of Privacy and Some Control

The day you go public, your company's inner workings become substantially more transparent. You must disclose financial results quarterly, along with other material developments. This means competitors can examine your financial performance, and you can no longer maintain business information privately.

As a founder, you also **cede a degree of control**. Major decisions might require shareholder approval, and your board of directors (likely now including independent members and investor representatives) gains increased influence. If you previously owned majority control, your post-IPO stake might be significantly reduced, meaning you could potentially be outvoted on important matters.

Some founders experience a sense of reduced agility—the organization might become more structured and less able to pivot quickly. This transition from entrepreneurial to corporate governance represents a significant cultural and operational shift.

Regulatory and Reporting Requirements

Public companies face substantial regulatory obligations. You'll invest considerably more time (and money) in accounting, auditing, legal compliance, and investor relations. There are costs associated with preparing annual reports, conducting shareholder meetings, and maintaining regulatory compliance (for instance, the Sarbanes-Oxley Act in the U.S. mandates strict financial controls and reporting processes).

These requirements can be **expensive and time-consuming**, particularly for smaller companies. For a growing business, this might feel like a distraction from innovation and operations. You'll need to develop robust finance and legal teams to manage these responsibilities effectively.

Market Pressure and Short-Term Focus

Once your stock actively trades, you receive daily feedback on market perception—reflected in your stock price. This can be energizing when the price rises, but challenging when it declines. Management may feel pressure to "hit the numbers" each quarter to meet analyst and investor expectations. This short-term focus can sometimes conflict with long-term strategic initiatives.

For example, you might hesitate to invest in a valuable long-term project because it would negatively impact quarterly earnings. Additionally, stock price **fluctuations can become distracting**—imagine arriving at work to discover headlines about your company's value dropping 10% overnight due to market rumors or broader economic concerns. Maintaining team focus on the mission rather than daily stock movements requires emotional resilience and disciplined leadership.

Ownership Dilution

An IPO inherently involves selling a portion of your company to new investors. Existing owners (founders, early investors) will own a smaller percentage after the offering unless they purchase additional shares during the process. While everyone's shares typically become more valuable due to the capital influx, the proportional ownership reduction can feel significant.

If not managed carefully, you might introduce shareholders whose priorities don't align with your long-term vision. The key consideration is that you're **welcoming new co-owners** who gain a voice in certain corporate matters.

Risk of Underperformance

Successfully completing an IPO doesn't guarantee ongoing market success. If the timing proves unfortunate or the company experiences operational challenges, the stock might underperform or even trade below the initial offering price (sometimes called "breaking issue"). This can damage morale and complicate future fundraising efforts.

Additionally, a **failed or withdrawn IPO** (where you begin the process but cancel it due to insufficient interest or adverse market conditions) can be detrimental, wasting resources and potentially harming the company's reputation. There's an inherent risk element—you're essentially placing your company's reputation directly in the market's judgment.

Despite these challenges, many can be mitigated with proper planning and expert guidance. Think of going public like relocating to a major metropolitan center: yes, the traffic is heavier and the pace more intense (drawbacks), but the opportunities and resources are significantly greater (advantages).

As a founder, understanding these trade-offs helps you prepare effectively. You might determine the benefits outweigh the challenges, or you might develop targeted strategies to address potential downsides (for example, investing in a strong CFO and legal team to manage compliance requirements, or cultivating a resilient company culture to resist short-term market pressures). There's no universally correct choice—the right decision depends on your company's unique situation and your long-term objectives as an entrepreneur.

The Post-IPO Identity Crisis

One of the least discussed but most significant challenges founders face after going public is what I call the "post-IPO identity crisis." After years of being the visionary rebel building something against all odds, you suddenly find yourself managing a public entity with formal processes, investor relations, and compliance requirements that can feel stifling.

A founder I mentored who took her cybersecurity company public described it this way: "The morning after our IPO, I sat in my office looking at the champagne bottles from our celebration, and I felt oddly empty. For seven years, every decision was about building toward this moment. Now what was I building toward? Who was I now that we'd 'made it'?"

This existential question hits many founders. Some respond by immediately looking for their next adrenaline rush—starting new ventures or making bold acquisitions that might not serve the company well. Others become overly conservative, so afraid of disappointing Wall Street that they stop taking the calculated risks that made them successful.

The founders who navigate this transition successfully find ways to redefine their personal mission within the public company context. They might focus on long-term innovation initiatives, mentoring the next generation of leaders, or expanding the company's social impact. They create new mountains to climb that align with both shareholder interests and their personal values.

If you reach this stage, prepare for this emotional adjustment as carefully as you prepare your financial statements. Define in advance what will keep you fulfilled beyond the IPO moment itself. Remember that going public isn't the end of your founder story—it's simply the beginning of an important new chapter.

The Investor's Lens: What the Market Looks For in IPOs

While you as a founder may view an IPO primarily as a capital-raising mechanism to advance your vision, **investors evaluate your company through a different lens**. Understanding what investors prioritize when considering IPOs will help you as a founder prepare effectively and present your company's story compellingly.

From an investor's perspective, an IPO represents an invitation to join a company's journey at a relatively early stage of its public existence. However, investors won't participate blindly—here are the key factors they typically assess:

Strong Financials or Clear Path to Profitability

Investors carefully analyze the IPO prospectus to understand your company's revenue trajectory, profitability (or losses), and growth patterns. If your business already generates profits, that's a significant advantage—it demonstrates a proven revenue model. If not, investors will look for a convincing path to profitability.

The "growth at any cost" mentality that sometimes prevails in private markets receives more scrutiny from public investors. In fact, public market participants generally **expect evidence that profits will materialize** in the foreseeable future. They will examine trends carefully: is revenue increasing substantially? Are losses narrowing? Essentially, they're asking: *"Will this business generate meaningful earnings, and if so, when?"* and *"Is the current growth rate impressive and sustainable?"*

A Compelling Narrative & Addressable Market

Numbers alone don't secure investment interest. Investors also want to understand your company's story and purpose. What problem are you solving, and how large is the potential market opportunity? If you can articulate a vision showing how your company could capture a substantial market segment or even create an entirely new category, that resonates with investors.

They actively seek companies with a **sustainable competitive advantage or unique innovation** that differentiates them from alternatives. Your business model should be logical and ideally demonstrate some defensive moat (characteristics that make it difficult for others to replicate or compete effectively).

For example, investors will be attracted to a biotech company with a groundbreaking treatment approach, or a technology firm with powerful network effects that competitors can't easily match. Show them that by participating in your IPO, they're securing a position in the *next significant development* in your industry.

"Markets invest not just in what your company is today, but in the story of what it can become tomorrow. The most successful IPOs paint a picture where current metrics are merely the opening chapter of a much larger narrative."

Trustworthy Leadership and Governance

Remember, when investors purchase your stock, they are essentially placing their trust in you and your leadership team to make sound decisions. Investors therefore scrutinize the **founders and management team** extensively. Your experience, strategic vision, and demonstrated integrity significantly influence their perception.

They also evaluate governance structures: is there a qualified, independent board of directors? Are shareholder rights appropriately protected? A potential warning sign for many investors is when founders retain disproportionate control (for instance, multi-class shares that give founders outsized voting power can concern investors unless there's compelling justification).

WeWork's failed IPO attempt in 2019 illustrates this principle—investor resistance stemmed partly from governance and leadership concerns. Public market investors "refused to embrace a growth narrative that wasn't supported by financial fundamentals and sound gover-

nance practices." This episode demonstrated that even a highly pro-
moted company can stumble if investors don't believe the leadership
will operate with broader shareholder interests in mind.

Therefore, *integrity, transparency, and a shareholder-focused approach* significantly enhance investor confidence in your offering.

Fair Valuation

Regardless of your company's quality, sophisticated investors will
question whether the IPO price represents reasonable value. They will
compare your company's financial metrics (such as earnings or revenue multiples) with similar public companies to determine if they're
paying an appropriate price. If they perceive the valuation as excessive
(meaning the IPO price seems difficult to justify based on fundamentals), many may decline to participate.

For founders, this highlights the importance of trusting your underwriters' pricing guidance—establishing an attractive entry price
helps ensure investors see potential upside. Many successful IPOs are
intentionally priced slightly below the company's potential full value
to provide that initial investor group with a compelling reason to
participate (a modest first-day price increase is generally viewed posi-
tively).

Investors are fundamentally seeking a **balanced opportunity**—they want to acquire shares at a price that allows for reasonable appreciation, not at a peak valuation that limits further growth
potential. It requires finding the right balance: not too expensive
(overvalued) and not too discounted (which might suggest problems
or unnecessarily dilute existing shareholders), but *appropriate for the
company's current stage and future prospects.*

Market Conditions and Sentiment

This factor extends beyond any individual company's control, but
investors carefully consider the broader market environment. Dur-

ing bullish periods when equity markets are rising, investors typically show greater enthusiasm for IPOs. During bearish conditions or when recent IPOs have underperformed, they become significantly more cautious.

They will examine how similar companies to yours have performed following their public debuts. As a founder, while you can't alter market conditions, you can strategically time your offering. Investors recognize suboptimal timing; sometimes even excellent companies postpone IPOs when markets become turbulent. Consequently, investors consider whether the IPO timing makes sense and whether broader trends (interest rates, economic outlook, sector performance) support taking a new position.

They'll also remain alert to excessive hype—if an IPO generates extraordinary publicity suggesting guaranteed success, experienced investors may adopt a contrarian perspective and proceed cautiously. **Sophisticated investors prioritize substance over promotion**: they examine the detailed disclosures and aren't influenced solely by brand recognition if the underlying metrics don't support the valuation.

In summary, investors seek a **balanced combination of growth potential and fundamental strength**. They want both logical and emotional engagement: the analytical side needs to see solid performance indicators and governance, while the visionary side wants to participate in something potentially transformative. As a founder, understanding these expectations allows you to better prepare your company to meet them.

By the time you conduct your roadshow, you should confidently address these considerations: demonstrate your business strengths, acknowledge risks transparently, and communicate that you're committed to building sustainable shareholder value, not just pursuing personal objectives. When investors recognize that alignment—that *your success = their success*—they're much more likely to support your offering enthusiastically.

Learning From History: Famous IPO Examples and Their Lessons

Many entrepreneurs before you have navigated the public markets—some with remarkable success, others with unexpected challenges. Let's examine several noteworthy IPO stories. These real-world examples provide powerful lessons that can inspire and guide your approach.

Google (2004) — Breaking Convention for Long-Term Vision

One of history's most influential IPOs was Google's in 2004. During this period, Google's founders Larry Page and Sergey Brin approached the process unconventionally. They selected an unusual auction-style offering method (a Dutch auction) to ensure fair pricing and broader access for retail investors. They also included an unconventional "Owner's Manual" in their prospectus, candidly telling potential investors that Google would prioritize long-term innovation over quarterly results—explicitly stating *"Google is not a conventional company."*

Initially, some Wall Street traditionalists questioned this approach. Google's IPO priced at $85 per share (considered aggressive by some), and didn't experience the dramatic first-day price surge that some had anticipated. But the profound lesson here is that **maintaining your principles can yield tremendous results**. Google demonstrated that with a compelling vision clearly articulated, the right investors will provide support.

Over time, Google's stock value multiplied many times over, validating their long-term focus. For founders, Google's experience teaches that you needn't follow every established convention if you genuinely believe in a different approach—but you *must* clearly explain your reasoning to earn investor trust.

Facebook (2012) — Overcoming Initial Adversity

Facebook's IPO was among the most anticipated of its decade, and it successfully raised substantial capital at an impressive valuation. However, the debut proved challenging. On the first trading day, technical glitches at the NASDAQ exchange disrupted order processing, and the stock barely moved from its $38 offering price. In subsequent days, Facebook shares actually declined significantly below the IPO price, leading many observers to label it disappointing.

It would have been easy to declare the IPO unsuccessful at that point. But here's the *motivational insight*: **a difficult beginning doesn't determine the ultimate outcome**. Facebook's leadership maintained focus on building the business—they improved their mobile advertising strategy (a major concern at IPO time) and demonstrated consistent user growth. Within a year, the stock recovered, and in subsequent years, Facebook (now Meta Platforms) became one of the world's most valuable companies.

The lesson for founders is resilience. The IPO represents just one day—what truly matters is *delivering on your promises afterward*. If your company creates genuine value, early market volatility can be overcome. Don't allow initial market reactions to undermine your confidence in your long-term mission.

"Markets are emotional in days and weeks, but rational in months and years. The true measure of an IPO's success isn't the first day's trading, but whether the company fulfills the promise that brought it to market in the first place."

Alibaba (2014) — Thinking Globally with Audacious Scale

Alibaba, China's e-commerce giant, executed what was (at that time) the **largest IPO in history**, raising an astonishing $25 billion. Investors were captivated by the sheer scale of Alibaba's market opportunity (hundreds of millions of Chinese consumers) and the visionary leadership of Jack Ma, a former English teacher turned tech entrepreneur. The shares were priced at $68 and ended the first trading day substantially higher, reflecting extraordinary demand.

Alibaba's triumphant IPO highlighted the power of a grand vision: Jack Ma consistently spoke about enabling small businesses and connecting global commerce. Alibaba's public offering also demonstrated **cross-cultural market appeal**—they listed on the NYSE in the United States, proving that global investors will support you if you present a compelling growth narrative, regardless of geographical origins.

For aspiring entrepreneurs, Alibaba's story reinforces the importance of **thinking at scale**. If your addressable market is substantial and you can articulate how you'll serve it effectively, you can attract massive support. It also reminds us that innovation and growth aren't limited by geography; transformative companies can emerge anywhere and still succeed on the world stage.

WeWork (Attempted 2019) — A Cautionary Tale

Not all IPO stories end in success—and there's tremendous value in understanding the ones that encounter difficulties. WeWork, a high-profile office-space startup, attempted an IPO in 2019 with a private valuation approaching $47 billion. However, when investors scrutinized WeWork's financials and governance during the IPO process, serious concerns emerged.

The company was experiencing multi-billion dollar losses with no clear profitability timeline, and its founder Adam Neumann had made questionable decisions (including having the company lease buildings he partially owned—creating potential conflicts of interest). WeWork's IPO met with such investor skepticism that it was ultimately **withdrawn**—the company had to cancel the offering, and its valuation plummeted dramatically in the aftermath.

What lessons can we draw? First, **public investors apply greater scrutiny** than private market investors—you can't assume that what excited venture capitalists will equally resonate with public markets. WeWork's business model and substantial losses didn't convince IPO investors who sought greater certainty of eventual profitability.

Second, **governance and transparency are non-negotiable**: WeWork's filing revealed governance issues (including special voting rights for the founder and potential self-dealing arrangements) that undermined investor confidence. The fundamental takeaway is that substance must support promotion. As a founder, ensure your business fundamentals and governance structures are robust before facing public market evaluation.

The inspirational perspective here is that while WeWork's initial IPO failed, it catalyzed necessary changes—new leadership took control, and the company refocused its strategy. Sometimes, challenging feedback from the market can drive improvements that strengthen the organization for the future.

Beyond the Headlines — Your IPO Story

Each IPO follows a unique trajectory, and while these examples represent prominent technology companies, thousands of businesses across various sectors have successfully gone public, each with distinctive characteristics. The common thread in successful public offerings is thorough preparation, transparent communication, and unwavering focus on creating sustainable value.

The common element in troubled IPOs usually involves disconnection between *expectations and reality*—either the company overestimated its readiness or misinterpreted investor priorities. By learning from your predecessors, you gain valuable perspective. You can approach your future IPO with both the humility to recognize it's a challenging path and the confidence to know it has been successfully navigated by entrepreneurs no more capable or passionate than yourself.

Use their experiences as guidance: emulate Google's principled approach to maintaining vision, adopt Facebook's resilience in overcoming setbacks, embrace Alibaba's ambitious scale of thinking, and heed WeWork's lessons about maintaining transparency and sound governance.

Emotionally, an IPO can be bittersweet for a founder. On one hand, it's often the realization of a dream—your company is *out there* and you might personally become quite wealthy on paper. Early team members and investors may finally reap rewards, which is fulfilling to see. On the other hand, you might feel a sense of loss. The tight-knit, us-against-the-world chapter closes. The company is no longer *just yours and your inner circle's*; it belongs partly to the public now. But remember why you did it: presumably to **take your mission to an even larger scale**. As long as you stay true to that mission, the IPO is just another platform to achieve it.

Public Purpose: "The day your company goes public, success is redefined. Your purpose isn't—or shouldn't be. Use your expanded platform not to chase quarterly numbers but to amplify the mission that inspired you from the beginning."

Motivational Insight: *"After climbing a great hill, one only finds that there are many more hills to climb."* — Nelson Mandela. In business terms, the IPO is that great hill—absolutely celebrate the accomplishment (you and your team earned it!), but stay hungry and humble for what's next. The journey isn't ending; it's entering a new phase. As one founder quipped, "We graduated—now it's time to go to work with the big boys." Keep your long-term vision in focus and don't let the quarterly rhythm erode the boldness and innovation that got you here.

What matters most in the IPO stage:

- **Operational Maturity:** Ensure your company has the **processes, controls, and people** to meet the rigors of being public. This means great finance and legal teams, clear internal controls, and the ability to hit deadlines (like quarterly reports) consistently. Essentially, you're proving to the world that your business isn't a house of cards—it's built on solid fundamentals that can withstand scrutiny.

- **Leadership & Communication:** As a public-company leader, communication is one of your top jobs. You must articulate your vision not just to employees and customers, but now to analysts, shareholders, and the media. Be transparent about challenges and honest in your successes. Internally, guard your company culture. Going public can introduce new distractions (stock price obsession, etc.). Reinforce to your team that *customer satisfaction, product innovation, and company values* remain the north star, not the day-to-day stock ticker.

- Staying True to Your Mission: With new pressures and voices now in the mix, it's critical to keep the "soul" of your company intact. The best public companies still behave like startups in the ways that count — they innovate continuously, take care of their people, and focus on long-term impact. Remember the why that started this whole journey. Wall Street's expectations come and go, but your purpose can remain steady. An IPO gives you capital and fame; it's up to you to use those for the benefit of the mission and not get sidetracked.

Exit: Successful Endings and New Beginnings

Every founder's journey eventually comes to an exit — a point where you, as the founder, step back or move on from the company you started. An IPO itself is one form of exit (at least for your investors, and potentially for you if you sell some shares). But not all exits are IPOs. In fact, many entrepreneurs exit via acquisition: selling the company to a larger player, or via other paths like mergers or management buyouts. In this stage, we'll explore what a successful exit can look like and how it feels from the founder's perspective.

Exit Enlightenment: "The most profound moment of entrepreneurship isn't when you start your company—it's when you let it go. This is when you discover whether you built an organization that transcends you or merely an extension of yourself."

One common exit path is an Acquisition — essentially, your startup is bought by a bigger company. This could be a full 100% buyout (you and all shareholders sell everything and the company becomes a part of the acquirer), or a majority stake purchase. Acquisitions can happen at any stage, but a "successful" acquisition usually means you grew your business to a point where a bigger industry player sees significant value in it — and offers a price that makes you and your investors very happy. For example, remember Instagram's story: they were only about two years old, with a superb app and a booming user base, when Facebook came knocking in 2012. Facebook offered to acquire Instagram for about $1 billion in cash and stock. That was a stunning number given Instagram had very little revenue at the time. The founders, Kevin Systrom and Mike Krieger, chose that exit because it allowed their creation to leverage Facebook's massive resources and user base — and indeed, under Facebook, Instagram skyrocketed to become a social media titan in its own right. This is a dream scenario for many founders: a big payday and the chance to see their product go further than they could have taken it alone.

My own exit came through acquisition rather than IPO. After scaling our healthcare scheduling platform to over two hundred hospitals nationwide, we began receiving interest from larger healthcare technology companies. At first, I reflexively dismissed these inquiries—my company was my identity, my life's work. How could I possibly let it go?

But a conversation with our lead investor changed my perspective. "An acquisition isn't the end of your vision," he told me. "It's a force multiplier for your impact. The right acquirer can take what you've built to places you couldn't reach alone."

When MedTech Solutions, a public healthcare technology leader, approached us with a serious offer, I viewed the conversation differently. Their distribution reached every major hospital system in the country. Their R&D budget was twenty times ours. Most importantly, their leadership shared our mission of reducing healthcare staff burnout through better technology.

The decision to sell wasn't easy, but it became clear it was the right move for our mission, our team, and yes, our investors (including myself). The $220 million acquisition price validated our work, but more meaningful was seeing our software deployed to thousands of additional hospitals in the following years, touching millions more healthcare workers than we could have reached alone.

The day we closed the deal was surreal—celebrating a tremendous achievement while simultaneously saying goodbye to my identity as CEO. In that moment, I understood that a successful exit isn't just about the financial outcome—it's about ensuring your creation continues to fulfill its purpose, even without you at the helm.

If you reach the stage of entertaining acquisition offers, there are several things to consider. Strategic fit is key: Why does the acquiring company want to buy you? Is it for your technology? Your team (sometimes acquisitions are basically talent grabs, known as "acqui-hires")? Your user base? Or to eliminate a competitor? Understanding their true motivation will help you negotiate and also judge if it's the right move for your vision. Ideally, the acquirer values what you've built and wants to nurture it, not just absorb and erase it. The best acquisitions are where $1 + 1 = 3$, meaning together, the combined entity creates more value for customers than either could alone.

Another consideration: Your role post-acquisition. As the founder, do you plan to stay on with the big company for a while, or are you looking to hand over the keys and leave? Many deals will require key founders to stay for at least 1-3 years to ensure a smooth integration. This often comes with incentives like retention bonuses or big-company stock grants. Think hard about this: going from running your own show to being a part of a much larger organization is a big shift. Some founders relish the new scale and learning opportunities; others chafe at no longer being in charge. There's no right or wrong feeling — just be honest with yourself about what you want. If you do stay, use that time to champion your team and product within the larger company. If you plan to leave sooner, make sure the transition is set up for success without you.

Financially, an exit is the payoff for all the years of hard work and risk. It can be life-changing for you, your family, and your early team who held stock. It's okay to enjoy that! But also plan for it wisely. Founders sometimes struggle after selling — suddenly your identity tied to the company is gone, and you're sitting on a pile of cash wondering "what now?" Many channel that into new ventures, becoming angel investors themselves, or pursuing passions that took a backseat (philanthropy, writing, traveling, etc.). It's a transition, and like any major life change, it comes with emotional complexity. One chapter ends, and a new one begins.

Legacy Lesson: "A founder's true legacy isn't measured in dollars from an exit, but in three dimensions: the lives you've improved through your product, the people you've developed through your leadership, and the example you've set through your journey."

Importantly, a successful exit is not just about the money; it's also about the legacy and lessons. Look at what you've created: jobs for your team, value for your customers, perhaps innovation in your industry. That doesn't vanish at exit — that impact is real and lasting. Even if the product you built is absorbed or sunset by the acquirer over time, the experience and growth you and your team gained are yours forever. You'll carry them into whatever comes next.

The Post-Exit Identity Vacuum

Perhaps the most challenging aspect of a successful exit is the sudden identity vacuum that follows. For years—sometimes decades—you've been "the founder of X." Your calendar has been packed with meetings, your phone constantly buzzing with urgent matters. Then suddenly, after the papers are signed and the money hits your account, the emails slow to a trickle. Your schedule empties. You're wealthy but, in many ways, purposeless.

This transition can trigger what psychologists call "sudden wealth syndrome"—a set of psychological challenges including guilt, isolation, and uncertainty about the future. I've seen brilliant founders become depressed after exits that objectively appeared hugely successful.

The entrepreneurs who navigate this transition well typically prepare for it in advance. They develop interests and identities beyond their company while still running it. They have clarity about what they'll do in the first six months post-exit—whether that's focused family time, philanthropy work, or early exploration of their next venture. Most importantly, they've built a support network of other post-exit founders who understand this unique psychological terrain.

If you're approaching an exit, remember this: the skills that built your company—vision, resilience, problem-solving—are transferable. Your entrepreneur's mindset doesn't disappear when your company does. Instead of viewing your exit as an ending, frame it as a commencement—a beginning of your next chapter with more resources, wisdom, and freedom than you had before.

Motivational Insight: "Don't cry because it's over; smile because it happened." This popular saying (attributed to Dr. Seuss) is a perfect mindset at the moment of exit. Yes, it can be bittersweet to let go of something you poured your heart into. But be proud of the journey you've been through and what you achieved. You've lived the dream that many only talk about — starting from an idea and seeing it through to a successful outcome. That's huge. And remember, every ending is a new beginning. You're not the same person you were at the start of this story — you're wiser, stronger, maybe a bit battle-scarred, but also battle-tested. The end of this venture could be the start of your next, with a fresh slate and a wealth of experience to draw on.

What matters most at Exit:

- Timing and Fit: If you choose an exit like an acquisition, do it for the right reasons. Is this the right time (have you maximized the value)? Is this the right partner (will they honor your product/team/mission)? A good exit leaves you feeling that the company will thrive in its next home, and that you secured the best outcome for your stakeholders.

- Taking Care of Your People: One thing founders often care deeply about is their team's well-being in an exit. Negotiate for your employees' roles or severance if you can. Make sure they share in the upside (through stock options payouts or bonuses). These people believed in you and helped build the dream — a win for you should be a win for them too.

- Personal Transition: Prepare yourself for life after exit. It can be a jarring change of pace. One day you're CEO; the next, you might have no emails flooding your inbox. Plan some time off to recharge — you've earned it. Reflect on what you want to do next (but no rush to decide immediately). Oftentimes, new ideas will start percolating naturally once you've had a chance to breathe.

Committing to the Journey Ahead

We've now traveled the entire arc of the founder's journey, from the first inkling of an idea all the way to a triumphant exit. It's a hero's journey in every sense — and you, the founder, are the hero of your own business story. By seeing this journey from start to finish, you can appreciate both how challenging and how rewarding it is. No stage is easy — each comes with its own trials by fire — but each stage also shapes you, unlocking new levels of growth, skill, and insight.

Journey Joy: "The entrepreneurial path isn't just about building a business—it's about becoming the person capable of building that business. Each stage reshapes you while you reshape the world. Embrace this transformation as the greatest reward of the journey."

As you contemplate someday ringing that ceremonial bell and seeing your company's name in financial headlines, keep these lessons in mind. Remain true to your vision (as Google demonstrated), prepare to adapt and persevere (as Facebook showed after its challenging start), think ambitiously (as Alibaba exemplified with its global aspirations), and maintain impeccable fundamentals and governance (learning from WeWork's missteps). Perhaps most importantly, nurture the right mindset. A founder who approaches an IPO with clear-eyed awareness—recognizing the challenges but driven by purposeful mission—will not only lead a successful public offering but also guide a thriving public company afterward.

"The best founders see an IPO not as the final chapter of their startup story, but as the prologue to an even more ambitious second volume—one where their vision can unfold at greater scale, with more resources, and impact more lives than ever before."

Your IPO, when that day arrives, doesn't represent the conclusion of your journey; it's a commencement in the truest sense. Just as a graduation ceremony celebrates past achievements while opening the door to future challenges, an IPO honors how far you've come and establishes the foundation for even greater accomplishments ahead.

Take a deep breath, continue learning and preparing, and when the timing is right, step forward with confidence. The world awaits your company—and you—at the next level of impact and growth.

Final Reflections: Your Entrepreneurial Legacy

It was a crisp autumn morning when I returned to the hospital where I'd once worked as a nurse—only this time, I wasn't there to clock in for a shift. I was there to donate the equipment that would become the foundation for a new innovation lab. As I watched the staff excitedly explore the technology my company had developed, something profound struck me: the value of what we build extends far beyond the balance sheet.

Throughout this book, we've walked the winding path of entrepreneurship together—from overcoming internal limitations to navigating the complexities of going public. We've discussed strategies, structures, tools, and techniques. But as we reach the end of our journey together, I want to shift our focus to something even more fundamental: what it all means.

Beyond the Exit

Many entrepreneurs fixate on the exit—that moment of vindication when years of work transform into financial reward. There's nothing wrong with this; exits often represent both achievement and opportunity. But I've found that the most fulfilled founders are those who see beyond the transaction to the transformation.

What transformation am I talking about? Three kinds:

First, the transformation of self. The person who begins an entrepreneurial journey is never the same person who finishes it. The challenges you face as a founder forge something new in you: resilience in the face of rejection, wisdom born from mistakes, empathy deepened by leadership. These qualities don't disappear when you cash the check. They become part of your character, enriching everything that follows.

Second, the transformation of others. Every venture touches lives: the employees whose careers flourish under your guidance, the customers whose problems you solve, the partners whose businesses grow alongside yours. I still receive messages from team members who worked at my first company twenty years ago, telling me how that experience shaped their path. Your impact on others will outlast any product you create or company you build.

Third, the transformation of possibilities. Each successful venture expands what's possible for those who follow. When you overcome an obstacle that others thought insurmountable, you create a new reference point. Your journey becomes evidence that encourages others to attempt their own. This is perhaps the most powerful legacy of all—the invisible permission you grant to future founders who will build upon what you've proven can be done.

The Courage to Begin Again

One of entrepreneurship's great paradoxes is that many of the most successful founders aren't satisfied with a single victory. Having tasted what it means to create something from nothing, they feel called to do it again. Not just for financial gain, but because the act of creation itself becomes a form of self-expression.

I call this the "founder's addiction"—not in a negative sense, but in recognition of how compelling the creative process becomes once you've experienced it fully. After my second company was acquired, I promised my family I'd take at least a year off. Six months later, I was sketching ideas for Treydora on napkins at our dinner table. My wife just smiled knowingly.

If you find yourself drawn back to the beginning—to that empty canvas where new ventures take shape—don't resist it. There's wisdom in this impulse. Each new project allows you to apply what you've learned, to avoid old mistakes while making fascinating new ones. The greatest entrepreneurs I know aren't defined by a single success but by a pattern of creation, learning, and creation again.

The Ethical Dimension

As we close, I must address something too often overlooked in entrepreneurial literature: the moral responsibility that comes with building something significant.

The tools we've discussed throughout this book—particularly AI—amplify your impact as a founder. They allow you to achieve more with less, to scale your vision further and faster than ever before. But this amplification applies to everything: your values, your choices, your oversights.

A company without an ethical core is like a ship without a rudder—it may move quickly, but its direction is determined by the prevailing winds rather than by purpose. I've watched promising ventures implode because their founders neglected this dimension, prioritizing growth at all costs only to discover that the costs included their integrity.

Ask yourself regularly: What values does my company embody? What lines would I refuse to cross, even for profit? How are we ensuring that our technology and business practices align with the world we want to create? These questions aren't tangential to success—they're foundational to sustainable, meaningful achievement.

Your Turn

As you close this book and return to the world of action, remember that theories and frameworks are merely tools. The real work happens when you apply them, test them, and adapt them to your unique circumstances.

You'll make mistakes—we all do. Some days, you'll question everything about your path. That's normal. The distinguishing quality of successful entrepreneurs isn't perfection but persistence—the willingness to learn, adjust, and continue.

I began this book with my story, but what matters now is yours. What will you build? Whose lives will you touch? What possibilities will you expand? These questions await your answers, not in words but in action.

The world needs builders who combine ambition with vision, technical skill with human understanding. It needs founders who see business not just as a way to make a living but as a way to make a difference.

It needs you.

So take what resonates from these pages, leave what doesn't, and step forward into your own entrepreneurial story. Whether you're starting your first venture or your fifth, remember that each journey begins the same way: with the courage to turn possibility into reality.

The future is waiting for what only you can build.

"The greatest use of life is to spend it for something that will outlast it." -- William James

AFTERWORD

CONTINUE YOUR JOURNEY

The Next Chapter Begins With You

Turning the last page of a book isn't the end of the journey—it's an invitation to start a new chapter of your own. The principles, strategies, and insights shared in "The Founder's Formula" are meant to be applied,tested, and adapted to your unique vision.

Deepen Your Growth at TreydoraVR.com

Ready to take your entrepreneurial journey to the next level? The conversation continues at **TreydoraVR.com** where you'll find:

-
- **The Founder's Formula Immersive   Course** – Experience the concepts from this book in our groundbreaking learning environment. Navigate virtual scenarios that test your   decision-making skills and reinforce key principles in a risk-free space.

-

- **Founder's Community** – Connect with like-minded en-trepreneurs applying these same principles. Share challenges, celebrate   victories, and find potential collaborators on our discord channel.

-

- **Executive Mentorship Program** – Apply for personalized guidance from Mark and other successful founders who have navigated the   complete entrepreneurial journey.

-

- **Implementation Toolkit** – Download practical resources including the Business Lifecycle Map, Funding Tracker, AI Implementation   Framework, and other tools mentioned throughout this book.

Your Invitation

Every great founder knows that reading about principles is just the beginning—the real transformation happens through application and iteration.

Visit TreydoraVR.com today and access your complimentary Founder's Digital Toolkit.

Share Your Story

Has this book impacted your entrepreneurial journey? We'd love to hear about it. Selected stories will be featured in our Founder Spotlight series and may even appear in future editions of this work.

"The greatest entrepreneurs don't just consume wisdom—they apply it, adapt it, and then create new wisdom from their unique experience. I look forward to seeing what you build." — Mark Loudermilk

ACKNOWLEDGEMENTS

A book, like a successful startup, is never a solo endeavor. I owe immense gratitude to the many people who made this work possible.

First, to my family, who supported me through the darkest times and celebrated with me during the brightest. Your unwavering belief in me has been my foundation. Thank you for your patience during the late nights of writing and your wisdom during moments of doubt. To my children, who inspire me daily to build a legacy worth passing on.

To my mentors—whose guidance on my first venture proved invaluable. You saw potential in me that I sometimes couldn't see in myself and provided both the challenge and support needed to bring it forth.

To the entrepreneurs who generously shared their stories and insights for this book—your transparency about both successes and failures enriches these pages immeasurably.

To my early readers and editors, who challenged my thinking and helped refine these ideas. Your honest feedback transformed this from a collection of personal observations into a comprehensive blueprint for founders.

To the team at Treydora who carried the torch while I stepped away to write—your continued dedication to our mission made this book possible. And to the thousands of users whose stories of transformation remind me daily why we do what we do.

To my publishing team, who believed in this project from its inception and provided both creative freedom and professional guidance throughout the process.

And finally, to you, the reader. Whether you're starting your first business or scaling your fifth, your entrepreneurial spirit drives innovation and creates opportunities. Thank you for allowing me to be part of your journey. I'd love to hear how these ideas impact your path—please consider sharing your story at treydoravr.com.

ABOUT THE AUTHOR

Mark Loudermilk is an entrepreneur, innovator, and mentor whose journey embodies the transformational power of resilience, continuous learning, and purpose-driven business.

Mark's path to entrepreneurship began in the most unlikely of places—a prison cell where, at age 19, he made the decision to transform his life through education and self-improvement. This profound personal transformation,detailed in the opening chapters of this book, laid the foundation for his unique approach to business: one that values service over self-interest, growth over comfort, and meaning over mere profit.

After rebuilding his life, Mark pursued education with remarkable intensity, earning degrees in Respiratory Therapy, Nursing, and Computer Science—often while working full-time in hospital emergency rooms and ICUs. For two decades, he served in high-pressure medical environments where split-second decisions impacted lives, an experience that honed his ability to remain calm under pressure and make clear-headed choices with limited information.

This combination of healthcare expertise and technical knowledge became Mark's entrepreneurial edge. His first successful venture was a healthcare scheduling platform that solved critical staffing challenges for hospitals.Starting with just a handful of clients, Mark bootstrapped the company to profitability before raising strategic capital that accelerated its growth into a nationwide solution used by dozens of major health systems.

Following a successful exit from his healthcare business, Mark founded Treydora, an innovative gaming company that merged entertainment with immersive storytelling. The platform continues to grow in its early stages. Through Treydora's sister project, TreydoraVR, Mark pioneered the use of virtual reality as an educational tool, creating immersive learning experiences that transformed how users engage with complex information.

Today, Mark divides his time between mentoring early-stage founders,strategic advising for technology companies, and speaking on entrepreneurship and innovation. He has directly invested in more than twenty startups, with a particular focus on mission-driven companies leveraging technology to address meaningful human problems.

Mark's philosophy of entrepreneurship, captured throughout this book,centers on a powerful belief: "The true measure of success is not how much you take, but how much you give back." This service-first mentality has guided all his ventures and remains at the heart of his approach to business building.

Mark continues to innovate through the Treydora University, where he develops immersive learning experiences and mentorship programs for the next generation of purpose-driven entrepreneurs. His work has been recognized with numerous awards, including the Healthcare Innovation Prize and the Ethical Enterprise Award.

Through his writing, speaking, and mentoring, Mark aims to equip the next generation of founders with both the practical tools and the mindset necessary to build ventures that are not just profitable, but meaningful.

"True success isn't measured by what you acquire, but by what you contribute and who you become in the process." — Mark Loudermilk